REAL ESTATE AGENT

*Not Only Professionalism.
Develop 7 Key Aspects of Your Career and Find Out
What People Really Need From a Real Estate Agent*

by George Tower

1

© Copyright 2020

All rights reserved

loss due to the information herein, either directly or indirectly. The author owns all copyrights not held by the publisher.

The information herein is provided for educational purposes exclusively and is universal. The presentation of the data is without contractual agreement or any kind of warranty assurance.

All trademarks inside this book are for clarifying purposes only and are possessed by the owners themselves, not allied with this document.

Disclaimer

All erudition supplied in this book is specified for educational and academic purposes only. The author is not in any way responsible for any outcomes that emerge from utilizing this book. Constructive efforts have been made to render information that is both precise and effective, but the author is not to be held answerable for the accuracy or use/misuse of this information.

Foreword

I will like to thank you for taking the very first step of trusting me and deciding to purchase/read this life-transforming book. Thanks for investing your time and resources on this product.

I can assure you of precise outcomes if you will diligently follow the specific blueprint I lay bare in the information handbook you are currently checking out. It has transformed lives, and I firmly believe it will equally change your own life too.

All the information I provided in this Do It Yourself piece is easy to absorb and practice.

Table of Contents

INTRODUCTION

Real estate sales is one of the greatest businesses inthe world when it comes to income potential. In any marketplace,a real estate agent has the opportunity to create hundreds of thousands of dollars in income. An agent's income is very important when compared with the capital investment required by the business.

In view of the recent advancement in technology across diverse sectors, including the internet and social media, a new agent can create the appearance of success, marketplace stature,and marketing experience, far beyond the early stages of a real estate career. This provides agents with better oddsat carving out a career for themselves.

Though advancement in technology has had an impressive influence on the real estate market in recent years, the basic skills of sales, marketing, time management and people skills have not changed that much.

This book is all about becoming successful as a real estate agent. It's also about acquiring the needed sales skills, marketing skills, time-management skills, people skills, technology skills, and business skills. It's about achieving more recognition, closing more deals, and making more money. It's a guide that helps you achieve the goals and dreams you have for yourself as a real estate agent.

If you make use of the information and knowledge provided in this book with the appropriate attitude, and if you are diligent in your practices as well as in your success expectations, your place in real estate agency is guaranteed.

CHAPTER ONE

Legal Requirement To Become A Real Estate Agent

A real estate agent is known for helping people to buy and sell homes or other related propeerties. He is a professional in the process of detailing a house to buy or working with a client to buy offers . Since agents are normally paid on commission, their pays differ considerably by property value and location.

Every state makes laws on the education, certification and other requirements for real estate agents.

Equally, every state has different legislations concerning real estate purchases, each state's regulation addresses requirements for professional licensing. Among such is to complete pre-licensing programs, which might cover real estate funding, agent conduct, title transfer, leases, property administration, and shutting a deal. On top of that, states might require that potential real estate agents be a specific age, have a diploma, or have sales experience so as to get a certificate.

Real estate agents are salesmen, but they are also involved in more consultative roles at the same time. They help sellers and buyers in completing a home acquisition deal and provide suggestions and advise as required. The capability to develop a good degree of relationship and trust with your client is crucial to continuous success in real estate. Each party relies on their agent to show understanding, connect factors associated with acquiring or marketing the home and knowledge on the whole process. In some circumstances, agents utilize even more assertive marketing abilities to get sellers to check with them or to encourage reluctant purchasers to make an offer.

Laws

A lot of the licensing training in real estate focuses on laws regulating the buying and selling of homes. Sellers are required to complete disclosure declarations to confirm or deny whether the property has had lead paint, experienced water damages or any other problem that might impact on the buyer's decision. Buyer's agents have to understand just how to properly complete an agreement or contract offer to buy, due to the fact that it is a legally binding document.

Buyers additionally need to authorize a great deal of disclosure documents and various other forms connected to the offer to buy.

Every state has its own distinct real estate laws, so it's crucial that individuals that wish to go after a real estate occupation acquaint themselves with the laws in their state. Regulations might control how homes can be bought, along with landlord-tenant problems, land usage, as well as building and construction.

There are some government laws that regulate just how real estate agents can note, reveal, and advertise residential or commercial properties available, so those that intend to get in the space must know.

Each state develops regulations on the accreditation, test, and learning needs of estate agents. Certain requirements differ substantially by state. Usually, you should conplete a real estate training program that involves a number of weeks or months of coursework. You take your state's licensing examination as soon as you obtain a certification of program conclusion. You have to fulfill your state's minimum passing rating needs. You can obtain agent's certification when you finish the examination. While some agents acquire associate or bachelor's degrees prior to entering real estate, this is not a common requirement.

Discover a real estate brokerage to collaborate with

New real estate agents are expected to work with a broker for at least two years after obtaining a certificate. Such company will look after all sales to guarantee they are managed within state and government standards. In many cases, individuals have to find a broker to deal with prior to taking their licensing test.

When searching for a real estate broker, take into consideration the company's track record, how it advertises residential or commercial properties, the area it offers, and the amount of agents that work there. Remember that you will likely be paid on a commission-only basis.

CHAPTER TWO

Laying Out The Blueprint

Positioning yourself against other agents

Knowing how your competition is performing and how you rank in the field is paramount to your success. Follow these steps:

- Learn the Big Three stats — average list price to sale price, average days on the market, and average listings taken versus listings sold — for other companies and agents. These numbers provide you with a basis for comparison and help you begin the process of positioning yourself and your company to the consumer.

- Define your competitive advantage. Keep in mind that how you state your advantage is often as important as what you have to say. How you present your objection and the level of confidence and conviction you have in your beliefs can make the difference between a listing and a futile effort.

- Convince your prospect of your advantage.

When I was a new real estate agent, the reasons I could present for why sellers should list with me certainly numbered fewer than later in my career, but that didn't stop me from securing listings — largely because my conviction about the advantage I offered sellers was so strong.

I told prospects that selling their home required a partnership with a focused, passionate, successful, sales-oriented agent. I explained that personal service, attention to detail, and creation and conversion of leads would sell their home, and that I was the agent for the job. I con- trasted myself positively with other, more-established agents by explain- ing that sellers hardly benefit from working with an agent who passes them off to interact with a series of assistants who handle the paper- work, marketing strategy, ad calls, sign calls, and open houses.

"Do you see the benefit of working with a person rather than this laundry list of underlings?" I would ask, before adding,

"Isn't this type of intimate relationship what you're looking for?"

My conviction regarding the advantage I offered sellers changed dra- matically after a few years in the business. By then I had assembled a service team and developed an excellent system for serving the client through others. My objection changed, as well. I explained to clients that one person couldn't possibly do with skill and precision all the activities that a seller needs and should demand from an agent. With so many hats to wear, a lone ranger agent can't possibly provide the level of exposure, communication, client service, and expertise that the team of experts I represented could deliver.

Both positions were truthful. Both had merit. The difference stemmed from my position at the time and the way I felt and articulated how that position benefited my prospects.

✓ Use numbers to demonstrate the clear advantage you present to clients.

Realize that if prospects can't see a clear difference between you and other agents, they will gravitate to the easy choice, which is to select the agent offering the lowest commission rate or highest initial list price.

Establishing Comparisms of sales and sales volume

Examining your efficiency against the statistics of other agents or companies in your market section is a great point to start base, but it's not only what you need to discover your unique advantage or point of distinction.

When you make comparism of your numbers to MLS statistics for the variety of systems marketed, variety of listings taken, variety of listings marketed, and complete sales quantity in your market location, you get a picture of how you did compared to the marketplace at overall. It's likely that your company is concentrated on specific sectors of the complete market- most likely you concentrate on specific areas, specific cost varieties, and specific types of homes.

To discover your edge or unique advantage, you need to segment the market-wide numbers. Possible ways of doing this include:

- You can reduce the geographic location down to a concise region or neighborhood as a way of comparing your own performance with the performance of market in that niche region.
- You can make analysis of real estate activity just in a certain price range.
- You can possibly expand the geographic space to include many neighborhoods in which you operate.
- You can concentrate on a segment that includes a particular type of property, such as waterfront homes or small multiplexes.

It is important that you should be fair and ethical when you decide to segment the numbers. You have to establish true comparisons and sincere evaluations of the sales volume and sales numbers and in each category you create. As far as you disclose the approach you adopted and define the segment you analyzed, focusing your main analysis on a specific segment of the market is a fair method of defining and presenting your strong competitive position.

Calculating per agent productivity

Most times, the largest company or firm in a market would account for the biggest sales numbers and sales volume, creating a strong market presence which eclipses the performance of individual agents and small companies. If you are faced with a David and Goliath situation, take steps to reach down and pick up the stone of per agent productivity in order to put in your slingshot.

You can calculate per agent productivity by dividing a firm's complete efficiency by the number of agents operating or working at the there. This calculation can be used to bring listings taken, listings sold, sales volume, total unit volume, or buyer- represented sales down to a per agent basis. With that, the "Goliath" won't look quite so oppressive or dominant.

Making use of market-area data to set your objectives or goals

It's important to always understand the average agent success numbers applicable to your market. These are the numbers you wish to eclipse by the end of your first six months in business.

Take time to know and understand the Big Three statistics and recognize specifically how your own productivity compares to market standards.

When the numbers are before you, you can compare your productivity to the market standard.

You can ask the following questions:

- What does not look good enough at first instance?
- If you widen or reduce the criteria, does your positioning get improved?
- Where are you falling back?
- How can you craft a position from where to sell if you're stuck to these statistics?

Increasing Your Share of the Marketplace

Nothing brings in business more conveniently than a dominant market share. When you boost your share of the pie to the point that it overshadows your competition, the expected prospects start to seek you out.

Determine Your Market Share

Market share refers to the percentage of sales that you control within your marketplace. It can be based on listings taken, listings sold, sales volume, buyer sales, or sales by units. In other words, your share reflects the portion of total market activity that is represented by you or your company.

How to calculate market share

To effectively calculate your market share, you simply have to divide your company's production level against the overall production recorded in your marketplace. For example, if 575 homes sold last year in your market area, and if your company sold 215 of those 575, then your company handled 37 percent of all transactions and controls 37 percent of the market activity $(215 \div 575 = 0.37)$.

You also need to calculate market share in various market segments, following the "slice and dice" advice provided earlier in this book. You might possibly discover that your overall market share happens to be low but you have an appreciable market share in a certain price category or neighborhood.

Inncreasing Market Penetration

This is another way to clearly describe market share. If you are in control of a large share of your market, you have achieved desired market penetration. Thus, if your market share is minimal, your penetration is also minimal.

Focusing on a niche market

Just one agent can't expect to individually penetrate a broad market overnight. A niche is a section of the total market. Niche marketing professionals serve a selected group of clients whose demands and passions are definitely different from the demands of the marketplace generally. Think about niche marketing professionals as big fishes found in small pond

You can develop a market niche by offering clients in a specific location, clients looking for a particular property kind, a specific sort of seller or buyer, a specific income classification, and the list continues. You can develop a particular niche by concentrating your initiatives and raising your infiltration of FSBOs, non-owner occupied properties, or little multiplexes.

Establishing Niche Penetration

The secret to getting penetration in a particular niche is focus. You need to choose which smaller section of the market you wish to function and stop attempting to become all things to all individuals. When you recognize your specific niche, you have to develop presence, penetration, and dominance, complying with these actions:

- **Establish contact with the prospects in your niche repeatedly over a specified period of time.**

Research has shown that it takes about six perceptions for a consumer to recognize or acknowledge who you are. By enhancing both the number and frequency of calls with leads, you can boost your market consciousness, which is a very first step in accomplishing market penetration.

- **Make individual contact**

  For the majority of agents, the prefered technique of contacting people in a particular geographical location is mail. They mail and mail their leads continuously. They send out refrigerator magnets; note pads with the agent's name and face; regional football game schedules; yearly calendar; and even more. That's insufficient to attain market penetration.

Treat It Like a Business

Just because real estate agents have a desk, on-the-job training, and guidance from a broker or manager, it doesn't mean they can afford to act like employees.

The fact that real estate is a time- consuming, all-encompassing type of job doesn't help either. Agents can literally spend all day answering phone calls, driving through neighborhoods, cruising the MLS for new and expired listings, and pressing the flesh with their contact base—all without generating any immediate income.

So many agents struggle with that mentally, and never quite grasp the fact that just because you put in the time, doesn't mean you're going to make money. It's important for all agents to create a business plan to avoid getting sidetracked by mundane, day-to-day tasks that don't generate income. Creating a business plan will significantly increase the odds of succeeding in the real estate business.

Business Sense

The correlation between thinking like a business owner and acting like a real estate agent is clear, but how does one go about adopting that mindset? Start by asking yourself the following questions that any new entrepreneur should consider before opening up a new business:

1. Am I self-motivated?
2. Am I a hard worker?

3. Am I an optimist and a risk taker, like most successful business owners are?

4. Am I a good problem solver?

5. Do I have the self-starter determination to get this business going, and the discipline and dedication to keep it on track?

6. Am I organized?

7. Am I willing to work weekends and evenings, when most home buyers are out looking at houses?

8. Do I have the stamina and desire to put in long hours?

9. Do I consider ethics and honesty to be important ingredients for a successful career in business?

10. Can I live on my savings and/or my partner's income for at least six to twelve months while I build this business?

11. Am I usually able to come up with more than one way to solve a problem?

12. Am I business savvy, or do I have a colleague or friend who can help me through the critical first few stages of business?

13. When I begin a task, do I set clear goals and objectives for myself?

14. Am I the kind of person whom nothing can stop once I decide to do something?

Don't worry if you didn't answer a resounding yes to every one of these questions, but if you were negative on five or more points, you may want to reconsider the small-business aspect of being a real estate agent. It's truly an entrepreneurial endeavor, particularly for the first two to three years, and a big undertaking that is not for the faint of heart. The sooner you accept this reality, the better off you will be. That means putting in long hours, operating on a lean and often fluctuating income, striving to find and keep clients, and even spinning your wheels a bit as you figure out what strategies work best so that you ultimately reap the rewards of your sweat equity.

To avoid unfavourable issues in your own real estate career, you'll need to organize your business approach. Start your own organizational journey with these seven easy steps:

1. Start at square one, like any new business owner would.

Instead of jumping right into selling homes, spend time planning, assessing, and researching before "opening your doors."

2. Identify what you're selling, to whom, and how you'll go about doing that.

3. Pick a specialty and stick with it. "No one should be a 'threshold' agent.

4. Attend local Small-Business Development Center (SBDC) seminars to learn how to start your own business, develop a business plan, and create a marketing strategy.

5. Track income and expenses. Use a program like Quick-Books basic accounting software and review monthly financial statements.

6. Name your business. Create a logo or identifying tag line, just as any new business would. In some states, due to licensing regulations, a business name may be for the agent's internal use only and not shared with the public.

Existing agents who need a refresher course on business ownership should take the same steps outlined above. No matter what stage of the game they're at, agents should revamp their internal image from 'real estate agent' to 'small-business owner.

To Incorporate or Not?

One way to really start feeling like a small business owner is by incorporating your business, although not all new agents will want to take this step fresh out of real estate school. Once the commissions start rolling in, you may want to join the ranks of business owners who have shed their sole proprietorships in favor of corporations.

Gene Fairbrother, lead small-business consultant for the National Association for the Self-Employed (NASE) in Dallas, Texas, says issues surrounding incorporation are a hot topic for his group's 250,000 members. "It's a major issue and the number one or number two question that our Shop Talk consultants work through with small-business owners," says Fairbrother.

Business owners are generally most concerned with which legal entity to select, afraid that the incorrect choice may hurt their companies. Basic choices include the partnership, the C corporation (a traditional corporation), and the subchapter S corporation. The corporation is considered by law to be a unique entity, separate from those who own it, according to the U.S. Small Business Administration.

A corporation can be taxed and sued, and can enter into contractual agreements. The shareholders of a corporation are know as its owners, as they have the responsibility of electing a board of directors to oversee the major policies and decisions. The corporation has a life of its own and does not dissolve when ownership changes. The S corporation is a tax election that enables shareholders to deal with the profits and earnings as distributions and have them pass through directly to their personal tax returns. The shareholders (if working for the company, and if there is a profit) must pay themselves and must meet standards of "reasonable compensation."

Another alternative is the limited liability company (LLC), considered as a "hybrid business structure which is now permissible in most states." The LLC is created to provide the limited liability features of a corporation as well as the tax efficiencies and operational flexibility of a partnership, though formation is more complex and formal than that of a general partnership.

For genuine estate agents, incorporating can be compelling, not necessarily for tax reasons but for the protection that such entities give to their investors. Operating in an increasingly litigious society, where real estate agents have become the target of claims varying from bad property disclosures to toxic-mold cases, some consider it a good idea to incorporate as a way to safeguard their properties from claims.

The following are reasons to incorporate a real estate business:

1. **Protection against personal liability**: If you run business in your own name, you are running the risk of losing whatever you have. A corporation will separate your business from your personal properties. If one of your workers commits a wrongful act, your corporation will be held accountable, but not you personally.

2. **Liquidity**: We all know of real estate companies having their owners' names all over them. Without that individual, the business has no name. The point is, you cannot sell a company if it relies solely on you. You need to establish an entity that differs from you that can be offered as an ongoing business.

3. **Less Risk of Audit**: If you are a property manager, a broker, or anybody else who reports income on a Schedule C, you are a high threat for an IRS audit. The IRS audits Schedule C businesses far more frequently than small corporations. Just by

incorporating, you might minimize your risk of an audit by as much as 300 percent.

4. **Tax Savings**: A corporation can be an outstanding tool for turning nondeductible costs into deductible costs. The old "home office" is a trap for small business people who attempt to declare the cost on their individual tax return. If your corporation rented the same location from your house, you lower the risk of being audited for the same deduction.

5. **Fringe Benefits**: Items like medical insurance, medical expenses, and life insurance coverage are not totally deductible as an individual entrepreneur. If you set up a C corporation, you can deduct 100 percent of your medical insurance coverage and medical expenditures, and up to $50,000 of term life insurance coverage. These benefits need to be provided to all of your full-time staff members.

6. **Income Splitting**: If you run as a sole proprietor, you are taxed on all earnings you make, even if you reinvest the money into business. A C-corporation is a different tax- payer from you. The corporation pays its own tax but generally at a lower rate than you pay (C corporation tax is just 15 per-cent as much as $50,000). You can efficiently minimize your total income tax if

you take a little income and leave the rest of the earnings in your corporation.

7. **Prestige**: In the business world, a corporate entity simply looks much better. People will think you are savvier if you are "North American Realty, Inc." instead of" John Smith Realty."

8. **Privacy**: A corporation offers privacy from spying eyes. It also provides you a buffer zone from your tenants. You wouldn't want your clients to know you are the owner. You are at a negotiating disadvantage when you are seen as the "greedy proprietor." Rather, you ought to represent that you are a staff of the corporation. That way, you are simply the "go between.".

9. **Portability**: Real estate can not rise up and leave. If a corporation owns your real estate, it can be moved quickly, given that the business stock can be moved. The ownership goes where you go if your real estate is owned in a corporation or other entity that has transferable ownership. This is essential in estate planning. Your successors need to go through probate procedures in each state if you own real estate in more than one state. By transforming the real estate into personal assets, there will be a requirement for probate just in the state in which you die.

Walk the Walk

By thinking and operating like a business owner, you'll be more apt to break out from under your broker's wing and start promoting yourself and your services by taking active roles in Realtor and related organizations, sponsoring events, and marketing yourself with a vengeance. Here are some other steps you can take to get yourself thinking like a business owner:

- Cut yourself a paycheck every week, two weeks, or month, instead of just dropping your commission checks into your personal bank account.
- Create an image for your business that includes your photo, logo, and a short tagline to use on all advertisements, correspondence, and other relevant materials.
- Investigate the possibility of incorporating, and research the various entities that are available to you as a real estate agent in your state.
- Get on a regular schedule of depositing estimated quarterly taxes.
- Adopt the philosophy that it takes money to make money, and don't be afraid to make affordable investments in

technology, tools, office supplies, or other materials that will help you reach new clients and/or retain the ones you already have.

- At the same time, keep tabs on your business expenses and spend only what your business can cover without putting yourself in the red.
- Operate with the highest of ethical and legal standards at all times.

If you've spent a lot of time working in a salaried or hourly position, handling these and other business-related issues will be quite a change for you. Take heed because you're certainly not alone.

It is important to take it step by step, knowing that as each day passes it will become easier and easier to adopt the mindset of a business owner, rather than an employee. If you need more help getting your business on track, try one or more of these business resources:

- Financial and Accounting Professionals: A quick review of your financial statements by a trained eye can help discover poor financial management, overextended accounts payables, slow collections, or other warning signs early enough. Financial advisers can help with providing similar services.

- Financial Institutions: Visit your bank for support with accounts receivable loan, a line of credit, or other vehicle to ease the cash crunch. Banks can also provide ancillary services for their small-business clients.
- Business Groups: Groups like the SBA, SCORE, and groups like the National Minority Supplier Development Council, Inc. offer programs and guidance for small-business owners with financial questions.

CHAPTER THREE

Designing The Client Experience

Your present client relationships will generate repeat business and significant referrals that draw in new clients into your organization when you provide exceptional service on a continuous and constant basis. As an outcome, your success will reproduce yet more success, your business will grow larger, and you'll need to offer exceptional service to an ever-growing group of individuals. Eventually, you'll deal with the challenging but essential job of transitioning from an individual service provider to a company which deals with a team to interact with and serve clients.

Transitioning from a do-it-yourself service delivery to a delivery that's executed through a team is an important turning point in an effective agent's business. It may also be considered as a complicated point. For these significant reasons:

- Even though you understand it's essential to leverage your business capability by designating jobs to others on your team, you might find it challenging to release ownership. This failure to let go can lead to service lapses and aggravation amongst clients and staff members.

- Unless you plainly develop and communicate your business philosophy and program to those on your team, you run the risk of providing an irregular or lower level of service to your clients.

The solution to both of these risks is to effectively communicate the kind of business or service you represent before you share responsibility for service delivery. To specify the level of service you desire your clients to get, respond to the following questions:

- **How often do you communicate with sellers?**

The primary grievance clients have about real estate agents isn't that they charge or make excessive money. The primary complaint is that they are irregular or bad communicators. Specifically if you're representing the seller, you need to know that your client desires consistent communication from you. You run the risk of a bad consumer relationship if you're not making a weekly call to offer an update on the process of the sale.

- How often do you make calls, send out e-mails, or e-mail reports?

- What is your procedure for sending out sellers copies of your marketing pieces for their property?

- Do you relay feedback to the seller immediately, or do you gather feedback to share in a once-a-week meeting?

- How frequently do you meet face to face, and do the meetings hold in the sellers' house or in your workplace?

- **How do you share and get feedback from provings?**

- Do you have a showing website or other software application that can provide the seller feedback from agents in real time, and do you provide sellers access to your marketing 24/7 simply by browsing the internet?

- Do you call the showing agent once, two times, or three times in hopes of a favourable response, or do you keep calling till you reach the agent and get feedback?

- Do you supply sellers with links to virtual trips or sites promoting their property? Do you make it simple for them to see, feel, and touch what you're doing?

- What actions do you require to expose the homes to cooperating agents?

- What systems or tools do you use to raise awareness of your property within the real estate neighborhood?

- How do you create awareness and interest within the general pool of real estate buyers.

- How do you promote the property online? What number of websites is the property marketed to, and can you quickly produce a traffic report to show the sellers?

- What marketing methods and systems do you use to bring in the right purchasers to your seller's property?

- In what order do you perform your marketing strategy?

When you are clear about what you mean and how you provide service to clients, you're in a position to train those on your team to serve in your place and to your standards. At that point, your shift from a one-person business to expert business orgaization is complete.

Promising, then perfectly delivering

The reality is, the majority of agents do not follow through with their promises for two significant reasons:

They over-promise, and thereafter they misplace what they promised they would do simply because they do not have a system to follow.

It's something to have a service delivery strategy or plan. It's another thing to execute your plan on a never-fail basis. There are variety of marketing plans from many agents out there. The majority comprise of 30-point, 50-point, or 100-point service action plan provided by the organization the agent works for or made by the agent in person. Experience has shown that a lot of them execute less than 30 percent of the points noted on their marketing plans.

Be prepared to under-promise and over-deliver

The difference between limited efficiency and outstanding efficiency does not originate from an abundance of wonderful extras. It's the result of keeping your commitments. For lots of clients, it appears it's rare to find a professional who keeps commitments.

Seeing your closing as a starting point, not just the finish line.

When the deal closes, great agents understand that their task isn't over. After you've accomplished the sale, sealed the deal, cashed the commission check, and spent the cash, it's time to begin strengthening your client relationship.

Sure, you would have to get on to the next income-producing activity. As you build your next offer, do not make the error of turning your back on the clients you just served.

Your clients might require more of your service after their closing than at any previous point in your relationship for any of the following important reasons:

- After moving into their new house, they might find repair issues that require attention. They might require the name of somebody who can repair their roofing, or they might require the names of service companies who are truthful, credible, and reasonable and who do quality repair. Connecting your clients with authorized suppliers, professionals, and providers is a great method of adding value to your service delivery.

- The taxes of their homes might be high as a result of the correction in value over the years. They might require you to assess the market, research similar homes, and provide a report of your findings that they can utilize as they contest their property's taxable value. This puts real money back in your clients' pockets.

- Your clients' home purchase might have triggered ideas about developing wealth through real estate financial investments. They might be thinking of how to effectively secure their retirement or how to create a savings for their kids's college education. If your clients see real estate as a piece in their wealth puzzle, they might seek your guidance about how to obtain and keep homes as an essential step towards wealth development.

- Your clients might simply have an interest in how the marketplace around them is doing. When you call them to talk, you're most likely to get the question, "How's the market?" or "What's going on in the market?" Now that they are home owners, your clients are vested in the regional real estate market. When they're prepared to make the next physical or investment move, you will become their resource and you'll be initially in line. You might wish to offer a continuous market update to all previous clients. This market update ought to reveal inventory, demand and supply numbers, and the significant opportunities in the market. It genuinely verifies the position that you're a market specialist.

Developing After-Sale Service

An after-sale service resembles a lot of things in life: People get thwarted before they take the initial step, and if they do not take the first step (the step that involves developing the plan they commit to follow) they can't start to meet their goal.

If you don't plan for it, aftersale service wouldn't just happen . You will most likely get so consumed with the preparation for the next deal and with the task of earning the next commission check that you'll overlook the opportunity to create long-term revenue through your past clients.

CHAPTER FOUR

Sales Expertise

Dealing with Sales Objections

Sales objection is actually part of marketing. For most individuals in sales, they offer an unmovable item in the way to your success. When faced with a sales objection, real estate agents usually freeze up. They do not know what to eventually say or do when faced with this threat.

Consider this principle: Sales objections are in fact, good. You can not offer anything substantial without sales objections Sales objections suggest a raised degree of interest, motivation, or desire to acquire what you're offering. Consider them as request for more information or details. The prospect is simply saying, "I require more details. If I appreciate the details you offer me, I'll deal with you." What can be better than that.

Delaying Objections

Among the very best methods to delay objections is to refer to your accepted agenda, stating:

"Mr. and Mrs. ABC, would it be okay if I answered your question when we get to item number five on our agenda? That's where we get to discuss"

In about 40 percent of the time, the sellers won't raise the sales objection again. You deal with the sales objection by smartly delaying its coming.

Strategically making use of your agenda to delay objections is very essential when the concern has to do with the recommended list price or the cost of your service. Do not respond to pricing concerns until you have determined the sellers' needs, wants, and expectations and you have also established the value of your service.

Steps for dealing with objections

Objections are quite inevitable, so you have to be ready to handle them followhng the four- step system described below:

Stopping briefly

When an objection comes up, listen to the client. Then, pause to quickly collect your thoughts and, for several salesmen, to reduce what might feel like high blood pressure. Pause to make sure that you listened to the objection completely. Do not attempt to shut or cut the individual off. Many salesmen are in the habit of interrupting as if they actually wish to pack the words back right into the client's mouth before they come out. This is the most significant blunder you can make. It shows disrespect and ignorance.

Acknowledging the objections

After listening to the objection and pausing to consider it, acknowledge the concerns identified. This serves as a confirmation that you clearly understand what was said by the client, and it also offers you a few moment to properly consider and prepare the right answer.

Take note, nothing in the above paragraph suggests that you must agree with what the client has said. You can politely acknowledge the concern and appreciate the client for bringing it up without saying that it's right.

You can acknowledge the objection by making use of any of the following phrases:

"That's a very interesting question. I'm really glad you actually asked it." "I understand where that might cause some challenges."

"I understand what your concern is in this area." "Tell me more."

Why do you feel that way?" "I can now see where that might cause you some concerns."

Isolating concerns

After acknowledging, you may be feeling ready to tackle the objections with your perceived best answers. Hold off a bit, if you can, while you proceed with isolating the concern. The process of Isolating implies asking: "If it were not for this concern, we would be working together, Is that correct?"

You encourage the prospects to lay all their concerns on the table by isolating. Through this significant step, you get learn and understand everything that is standing as an obstacle between you and your desired outcome.

Use any of the isolation scripts stated below as you help sellers express their concerns:

"Is this the only concern that prevents you from moving forward with my offer?" "Suppose we could actually find a suitable solution to this crucial concern of yours. Would you all us proceed?"

"If this concern didn't exist, would you be set to proceed with the deal right now?"

By effectively isolating the concern, you would learn exactly what you are up against. You may discover another objection in that process, which is the reason many agents avoid taking this step- but you would have to be faced with the objection later anyway.

Reacting with self-confidence.

Now you've listened to the objection, stopped briefly or paused, acknowledged, and isolated, It's now time to respond.

The most commonly raised objections have something to do with the agent's commission, the length of the listing term, the recommended list price of the specified home, and the need for additional time to make the listing decision. Over 80 percent of the objections you will encounter over the course of your career as a real estate agent stem from these major concerns.

You need to prepare yourself by outlining properly and mastering responses that effectively convince sellers you have the ability to handle the concern better than other agents.

Ask your broker to provide you with the scripts the company recommends for effectively handling sales objections. If the said company does not have them, you may choose to make an investment towards enhancing your career and buy them from an expert.

CHAPTER FIVE

Marketing Principles

Many real estate agents understand little concerning the market in which they function. This is one vital reason that clients believe they understand more than—ort least, as much as-- their agents do and why they do not hold their agents in high regards. This is particularly real with the limitless accessibility to real estate details in our new technical world. Clients can now access details and perform real estate searches without an agent ever knowing that they're doing their own research.

Clients can utilize a range of information resources to get all type of information on virtually any kind of property. A purchaser can touch right into Zillow (www.zillow.com) and gain access to the background of a property, find the previous acquisition rate, make note of the existing tax obligations, and sight airborne maps and satellite photos of the property. Clients can also access info concerning pre-foreclosure, disstressed, and repossession buildings.

You can offer yourself a liittle over different other agents and establish yourself as a local real estate specialist merely by doing your research, investigating your market location, and obtaining a mutual understanding of the facts that impact the real estate choices of your sellers and buyers.

Understanding the Facts That Control Every Real Estate Market.

Whether you're in a significant city market or a village, and no matter the country, the economic situation, and even the day and age in which you're working, when you're in the field of real estate, three core regulations apply to your business operation:

1. Real estate is controlled by the legislation of supply and demand. This guideline is outright and without exemption. The recognition of a market, the assumptions of sellers and buyers, and the rate of market sales are all determined by the supply of, and the demand for real estate available.

For example, recently, we saw fast admiration and a crazy reaction by clients in the U.S. real estate market from 2002 to

2007. This feedback was triggered by the truth that real estate demand went to an all-time high while the supply was restricted. This created quick admiration, with home sellers obtaining numerous deals within days and even hours. At once throughout that duration, homes in southern California were offering, usually, at 18 percent over the market price (the outcome of a market problem where demand overtook supply

The reverse took place right after bubble ruptured in 2008. The financial problems really did not help, but the real estate market made a huge change because supply overtook need. As a real estate specialist, you have to plainly recognize supply and demand levels and check them at all times.

2. Real estate is regulated by the legislation of domino effect. Place in different ways, favorable circumstances create favorable end results, and vise-versa. Dynamic financial development leads to a lively real estate market and solid gratitude of homes, while work loss and a negative economic climate create precisely the contrary result.

Before the current financial downturn, the schedule of loans with less documents demands and for clients with reduced credit rating resulted in a boost in clients that can get home mortgages. Financial institutions provided these loans, and then economic markets got the repackaged loans.

Several clients took on a lot more home mortgage financial debt than they might truly pay for. This developed an ideal tornado, with financial institutions needing to confiscate on a large number of houses. This developed a result of rate devaluation, such that an increase of investor purchasers is currently driving the reduced sector of the real estate market. Investorsnow represent over 30 percent of all homes marketed, although the historical number is less than 10 percent.

3. History will most likelyrepeat itself. Every industry has cycles. Durations of quick real estate recognition are followed by static periods wherevalue increases or drops. By obtaining industry knowledge or understanding, you can visualize fads both for your very own advantage and for the advantage of your clients.

By recognizing your market and viewing local statistics, you're aggressive and ready. The focushelps you get the needed details.

A couple of years earlier, 40 percent of new home mortgage were created as reduced- money-down, interest-only home loans. These limited-equity setting acquisitions were made on the assumption that the current rapid-appreciation cycle would actually continueand real estate rates would go up. That pattern was unsustainable, and the cycle eventually ended. A new cycle started, in which some markets saw a 50 percent decrease in the value ofhomes. Now, a new cycle has started, and costs are beginning to increase once more.

Obtaining Knowledge about Your Market

Real estate is like any other form of affordable venture. If you figure out all there is to understand about your area of interest, you'll derive an affordable benefit that will distinguish you from the competitors and develop the basis of your success.

Consider your market as your area of interest, like how a professional athlete sees a football field, basketball court, or hockey rink. The much better you know fully about that playing area, the much more you can manipulate it to your benefit.

Accumulating market information

One of the most difficult element of getting market expertise is figuring out whatfacts to gather and where to discover the details you require. A number of conveniently obtainable sources are readily available to Realtors. All you need to do is get in touch with the ideal individuals and make the ideal inquiries.

Your regional board of Realtors

All expert agents come from Realtor organizations that assemble and offer a wealth of analytical information. The facts you are able to acquire from your regional board consist of:

- The number of agents working in your market: This information helps you understand your competitive arena. It also enables you to track whether your competition has expanded or contracted. In the past few years, the number of agents in every marketplace has fallen dramatically . . . good news for you.

- Experience levels of agents in your field: Most boards of Realtors keep information regarding the percentage of agents recently licensed and those with three, five, and ten years in the business. This information provides you with another factor against which to measure your competitive position. Experience levels are currently rising because so many less-experienced agents exited the business in the downturn.

  Meet with the executive director of your local board of Realtors to discover the extent of the information that is available to you, how frequently new research is released, and how you can obtain copies for your ongoing review.

- The production of the average agent in terms of units and volume sold: By obtaining this information and comparing it with your own production units and volume, you can contrast your performance against the other agents in your local board. This information is useful in your effort to calculate your share of the market.

It also helps you understand how you stack up against the other agents your prospective clients might be considering. The average per-agent production is a key comparative statistics to use for marketing and positioning yourself in your local area.

Your local multiple listing service

The multiple listing service, commonly called the MLS, keeps statistics for all the listings and sales in your area that are processed through the MLS.

Due to the fact that some sales bypass the system, the MLS does not cover every sale. Typically, new construction contractors do not send their stock to the MLS, and several for-sale-by-owner (FSBO) residential properties do not show up on the list, either. Representatives occasionally offer buildings themselves or internal, and those sales often aren't sent to the MLS. In some markets, the supply is so reduced that sales occur before a home strikes the market. The MLS in the majority of markets covers even more than 95 percent of all market sales, and it stands for the best sign of real estate task in your area.

The MLS provides you crucial market data, consisting of:

- Average variety of days on the market
- Listing-price to sale-price proportions
- Listings-taken to listings-sold proportions
- Geographically energetic markets inside your solution location.

The NAR also performs yearly studies and research studies of vendors and purchasers. It looks into why clients pick specific agents; what solutions they look for from agents; and what geographical locations, and home services they seek. This kind of expertise allows you to offer the highest degree of advise and value to your clients.

The NAR likewiseinvolves records on 2nd home markets, investment homes, funding choices, and lots of various other subjects. It's one of the most effective solutions that NAR gives, however it's the solution that agents make use of the least. Make on your own an exemption and study this deep pool of information.

Its Realtor Online Magazine gives a nationwide sight of real estate sales: what's occurred in regards to sales and days on the marketplace, what individuals are buying, what funding they are making use of, what issues are arising, and what forecasts professionals are creating about the future. This is an effective device in the hands of an effective agent. Place it right into your decollection right away if you aren't presently obtained reviewing it.

If you live in a state where the give title insurance coverage to clients, the title business frequently perform market-trend records that enable representatives to much better comprehend the market in which they operate

Various other resources of market information

Consult your broker regarding company-compiled statistics on local issues and additionally on your company's market share and market infiltration. Specifically if you benefit a nationwide or local real estate business or franchise business, your company has most likely appointed researches that work to your reality-Collecting initiatives.

The National Association of Realtors

You can access a variety of nationwide sources to acquire a wide range of understanding. The very best is the National Association of Realtors (NAR), which creates some terrific research studies, records, and market data that a lot of agents never ever utilize.

Almost all real estate agents acknowledge the MLS for its substantial function in boosting communication and direct exposure of real estate homes. Less agents identify the MLS for its effective but underutilized role in reporting efficiency of agents, business, and parts of the market. Access and use this details to workin your benefit.

Analyzing the facts and numbers

When you have accessibility to strong facts and numbers, it's time to translate your findings to show up at final thoughts that guide your service in the appropriate directions.

The details you look for and assess respond tothreevital questions:

- What proximate real estate markets are affecting your market location?
- What migratory patterns is your market location experiencing?
- What market facts are you seeing that can help you prepareyourself and your clients for success?

To figure out exactly how nearby local markets are influencing your market location, research migratory patterns and afterwards research the factors behind the populace movements you find.

Identifying the impact of various other local markets

Real estate in your market location is largely affected by impacts beyond your own location.

Examining populace movement patterns

To measure populace movement patterns that influence the sellers and buyers pools in your market location, identify the response to the following questions:

- Is your industry expanding in populace or shedding populace?<br
- Where are new locals originating from geographically?
- Where are present citizens going when they move away?
- At what price are individuals showing up to or leaving your location?
- What financial variables (for instance, joblessness, newbusiness startups, price, or service sales development) are driving populace changes in your market?
- Are individuals moving right into your location or leaving your location?

Capitalizing and recognizing on market patterns

To clearly know and understand your industry and its financial problem, you may compare existing market task with related data from the previous year, making use of required standards.

If your responses lead you to think that a populace boom is pending, prepare yourself and your clients to benefit from a sellers' market and the positive results of a high-demand, low-supply market circumstance.

Alternatively, if your responses lead you to think that a populace exodus is starting to occur, you can guide sellers and buyers choices with that said expertise in mind.

- Compare the variety of sales and overall sales quantity, on both a year-to-date and year-to-year basis. This actually helps you recognize and anticipate issues in your market.

- Is the differencein sales rising or going down?

- Is the total sales volume rising or dropping?

- Is the variety of listings up or down? Less listings suggests a sellers' market; while more listings suggests a buyers' market. Are there essentially competitors for buyers than in previous years?

- Is the market ahead of or behind the speed of sales from the previous year?

- Compare the variety of listings taken. The offered supply in a market is the supply fifty percent of the supply-and-demand formula.

- Is the option much better for purchasers than in recent times?

- Is the supply of homes up for sale expanding or reducing when compared to this time around a year ago?

- Compare the average price of past years to this year's average sale price. Identify your market's ordinary price by separating total sales earnings by the number of homes really marketed.

- Is the average price rising or going down? If a marketplace is vibrant and healthy, the average sale price will be increasing.

- Is your market decreasing or increasing in value? For example, if the average price has gone from $249,000 to $257,000, your market is increasing in value. Realize that the ordinary price should be seen at the very least a quarterly basis. A one-month change in this particular figure does not suggest a lasting trend. This is specifically real in small market areas.

Furthermore, you need to observe the mix of sales. If a large volume of high-class properties sells in a particular month, those sales are able to have huge influence on the average sale prices for the period. Don't make assumptions based solely on a rise in the average sale price; be sure to check the mix of inventory to confirm.

- How well is the stock of homes aligned with demand? The supply level is possibly lower than the demand for homes if you have an appreciating market. In a depreciating or low level market, the stock or supply possibly surpasses the demand.

- Compare the level of appreciation of average sale price this year as against last year .

- Is the level of appreciation reducing or increasing when compared to this time around last year.

- Is the market obtaining stamina in gratitude or shedding its strength?

To comprehend your market and its financial situation, make a market-trend evaluation by comparing present market activities with related statistics from the previous year.

Putting together a marketplace evaluation

Before commencing your own market evaluation, check to see whether your regional board of Realtors or MLS puts together regular monthly reports about your marketplace. You can actually save yourself much time by making use of the data they offer on the available houses to buy in your location.

If the crucial information isn't readily available, then sharpen your pencil, clear some schedule time, and prepare to make an evaluation by yourself just by compilingfacts and numbers on a month-to-month basis.

1. Segment your market by location.

You need to get both a macro and micro view of the entire market and of selected area or school boundry locations. The wider view is helpful, but the close-in sight on certain location is crucial when you're showingspecific homes to clients.

2. Figure out available Inventory level

Know and understand the level of competition for your buyers' money by keeping records of the number of active prices on the market. In most normal marketplaces, about 55 – 61 percent of the inventory will sell on a yearly basis. When inventory levels are extremely low, these percentages can climb higher

On average, even a healthy marketplace will sell less than 15 percent of the available homes on a monthly basis. That monthly sale number happens most frequently in the spring market months. The market's inventory levels affect these sale percentages.

3. Effective Marketing of Yourself and Your Properties

Marketing is the one subject that gets all agents to pay attention. It's a large area that takes some time, cash, and a virtually overwelming number of choices. Marketing, as it ought to be, is high up on the order of business of anybody trying to make a sale.

A lot of agents invest more time worrying and asking themselves how to market than they invest in actual marketing. And the confusion is solid. The options you deal with as an agent are virtually without limitation, and you need to compete with other firms that market to clients every day. Daily, clients are swamped with tv and radio commercials, newspaper publication ads, direct-mail advertising and marketing, internet marketing, social-media marketing, and many other marketing messages.

The the best strategy for dealing with this is to focus. It's important to focus on what you desire to accomplish, what you would like to communicate, and your target audience.

At its core, real estate marketing is just an issue of communicating a message regarding what you have to a target market that might or might not desire what you're offering.

4. Changing from Print to Online

Before you invest any money, take time to set up a system for monitoring results. It makes little or no sense to throw money at any lead-shortage issue without having the ability to measure whether the new strategy is adding real money to your account.

What a lot of agents don't understand is that sellers are really engaging them to generate leads for their property. That's the first step in marketing their home. If you do that well, you increase the odds of closing the deal. You also benefit from the many new leads you create when you discover that some buyers don't want this seller's home but need help finding something else. The marketing you do for a property can generate a broader lead opportunity.

Set up a spreadsheet to monitor lead sources from all of your marketing efforts, both online and offline. If your marketing has a strong call to action that asks prospects to text or call in a response, using a call-in system like Google Voice for each of your major marketing efforts is advisable. Here's how the system works: For example, if you send out a direct-mail piece to homeowners who are delinquent on their mortgage to offer help in selling their home, you can set up a Google Voice number for that specific marketing piece and have it forwarded to your cellphone. When you pick up your phone and see the number, you would know a distressed homeowner is calling for help. Track these calls as they come in to monitor the effectiveness of each marketing piece — in general, the more calls you get, the more effective the piece.

5. Targeting Your Marketing Message

Just as important as where you put your marketing dollars is how strong your message is. Agents take up the wrong marketing road at that point when they attempt to take communication shortcuts by flooding the market with their ad messages. This particular road leads to a dead end for two significant reasons:

- You don't have the budget of a major national corporation, so you can't compete well in the mass-media environment.
- Your prospective client is already drowning in marketing messages. Another attempt by you to send another ad missile into the marke spaceis surely not the way to get the interest of that person you're trying to reach.

As a result of the successful efforts of media salespeople, agents get roped into spending huge sums of money on brand-building or image marketing campaigns that reach large, untargeted groups of consumers and that produce zero sales results. You have to establish a name and presence before this type of marketing works.

Successful Agents may seek to reinforce their dominant positions in the market and enhance their reputations by moving some of their marketing funds into image marketing. However, as an agent just starting to ascend the ladder of real estate success, image marketing isn't exactly what you need.

At this stage in your career, it isimportant that you reach highly targeted prospects with the right messages about particular offerings that suits their needs and interests.

As you plan your marketing communications, think in terms of who, what,and why: Marketing communications is anything that you mail or email to the general public, your sphere of influence, or current and past clients. You should have a plan and a specific goal before you proceed or hit "send."

- Who is your desired target audience?
- What exactly are you offering to your identified target audience?
- Why is the offered product a good fit for the needs, wants, and purchase abilities of your target audience?

6. Defining the scope of your target audience

Before you decide on how you will communicate your message and what exactly you are going to say, you have to know who you are trying to talk to.

The single most common mistake in real estate marketing, (just like other forms of marketing) is that marketers choose to create ads without a clear idea of the people they are trying to influence. As a result, they use the wrong media, say the wrong things, and fail to inspire the right outcome.

7. Positioning your offering

In today's cluttered marketing environment, consumers are trained to tune out messages that don't seem to address their real and unfulfilled wants and needs. In other words, if your message doesn't clearly deliver a solution to your prospect's exact problem — if it doesn't position itself into an open slot in your prospect's mind — then your money, efforts, and time will go down the marketing drain.

Positioning is the marketing art of knowing what available space or position you and your offering fill in the market and then getting that message to exactly the people who want what you're offering.

By first figuring out the position your offering fills, you can easily decide who you want to talk to, what you want to say, and what marketing vehicles — from advertising to direct mail to online to personal calls — you need to use to reach the people you're targeting.

8. Positioning the property you're selling

Understanding your product position can make the difference between reaching your targeted prospect and not, between motivating interest and action and not, and between making a sale and not.

In real estate, price is the cornerstone of positioning. In my experience, 85 percent of your marketing strategy is actually set during the presentation when you and the seller reach an agreement on the right price and, therefore, the right market position for their home.

After you've worked with a seller to agree on the right listing price, your marketing strategyis naturally brought into operation following these steps:

- Creating a description of the home's likely buyer
- Listing the home's benefits and the reasons why likely buyers won't want to let the home go to anyone else

- Selecting media channels or communications approaches that are most apt to get your marketing message in front of your target audience of likely buyers

Having Knowledge of your product position as well as the nature of your likely buyer places you in a better position to choose the right media channels to carry your message to your market. Consider the following generalities in your planning:

- If you're marketing a lower-end home in your marketplace, many of your prospects may not be technologically savvy. With limited resources, they probably haven't invested in the latest technology. They may have standard cellphones rather than smartphones. Their Internet connection may be slow.

A segment of these group of buyers that is tech savvy is the first-time-buyer category. Young buyers may have limited funds, but they spend those funds on gadgetry. They may be eating macaroni and cheese morning, noon, and night, but they have the latest smartphone that came out last week.

- If you are marketing a home in the mid-price range, you can be fairly confident that your prospects are somewhat Internet savvy. Research shows that over 90 percent of middle-income home shoppers have Internet access and that most make the Internet their home-shopping commencement point. To reach this audience, an effective Internet marketing strategy is very important.

- If you're marketing a high-priced home, one-to-one communications may be the most effective tactic. Sometimes because of time con- straints these buyers are using technology effectively but aren't on the cutting edge. In some cases they have people who do that for them. With highly-priced properties, you may find that mailing a high- quality brochure to carefully selected prospects nets greater success then your Internet marketing. Buyers for a property in this market posi- tion are likely too busy to spend hours on the Internet poring through properties. Additionally, many are connected with agents, so your other approach may be to market to agents directly.

Product positioning mostly works if the home you are selling is appropriately priced. If you give in to a seller's desire to set an unreasonably high listing price, your marketing task becomes more difficult because:

- You'll be forced to market to the wrong audience. In order to reach buyers who can afford the price the seller is asking, you'll be talking to people seeking a higher-level home than the property you're offering.

- Your product will lose in competitive comparisons. It won't take long for buyers to realize that the home you're offering is inferior to others they can buy with the same amount of money.

When you list an overpriced property, you have only two hopes for success: that the marketplace will heat up dramatically and lead to escalating prices, which brings your listing price in line with others, or that your seller will agree to a rapid price reduction.

CHAPTER SIX

Sustained Business Planning

In their quest to handle the day-to-day real estate tasks, keep those commission checks coming in, and manage a plethora of new and existing clients, real estate agents tend to woefully neglect themselves. Because no employer is socking away money for them in a retirement account, providing health insurance benefits, or giving them stock options, agents who overlook this aspect of their business can find themselves in trouble down the road.

To determine if you are one of these agents, answer yes or no to the following six questions and check your score at the end:

1. Is there a mechanism in place for investing in my future?

2.. Do I have life insurance?

3. Do I have health insurance coverage for myself and my family (if applicable)?

4. If I have children, have I established a means of investing for their college education?

5. Do I have a means of providing long-term care for elderly family members, if necessary?

6. Have I sat down with a financial planner within the last five years to discuss my nest egg and other relevant financial topics?

Scoring:

5–6 yes answers: You're well on your way to having a solid plan in place for your future.

3–4 yes answers: You're getting there, but you'll definitely want to look at some of the "no" areas to see where you can beef up your long-term planning.

1–2 yes answers: Time to take a step back from your day-to-day workload and do some long-term financial planning for yourself and your family.

If your score wasn't up to par, you're not alone. Most financial professionals know that inadequate long-term planning is endemic among small-business owners, including real estate agents.

Successful real estate agents tend to have a consistent internal wiring that allows them to prosper, regardless of market conditions or the economy. They react quickly, focus on client needs, and even place those clients' needs ahead of their own. Unfortunately, these business strengths can also be weaknesses.

"Real estate agents tend to subordinate their own business-, financial-, and life-planning matters to the practice of real estate," says Arzaga, a former real estate professional who often works with agents and brokers, helping them create long-term plans for financial success. In doing so, he's noticed that real estate agents postpone personal financial planning meetings at least five times more often than non–real estate clients, mainly because they're spending time on listing presentations, open houses, and mailings.

On the bright side, Arzaga says real estate agents have access to significant benefits that other small-business owners may not have at their fingertips, including:

- The ability to distinguish themselves strategically by creating a network of resources for their clients

- The ability to be well versed in investment real estate and serve a niche that is sorely lacking

- The ability to build a long-term referral business to ensure long-term value for their practice

- The ability to scale their business up (or down) while keeping a tight lid on expenses

- The ability to move their business fairly easily if it suits them.

- The ability to be extremely aggressive in their retirement planning

The irony is that many successful agents who have been in the business a reasonable amount of time desperately look forward to cutting back their work, or getting out of the business entirely. Yet, very few know what that looks like financially. "Very few people (and even fewer agents) understand the financial capital needed to maintain their existing standard of living during financial independence (retirement)," Arzaga states. "And even fewer understand the impact of taxes, inflation, Social Security, or working part-time."

The statistics prove it: According to AARP, 80 percent of people age 65 or older are unable to maintain a comfortable standard of living for themselves. Most find themselves looking for more affordable places to live, dramatically cutting expenses (very tough to do at that stage in someone's life), or working part- to full-time to meet their needs.

Indeed, real estate agents need to begin their long-term planning well before they're no longer willing or able to work. The longer the time horizon to financial independence, the more options and alternatives the agent has.

Early Steps

To create an effective long-term plan for personal and financial success in real estate, you'll want to revisit some of the basic business planning concepts covered in this book. Here's a synopsis of the key steps you should be taking:

- Make sure you go into the business with your eyes open, and with the support of your significant other.
- Create a business and marketing plan that is attainable and that creates accountability.

- Make sure your current financial condition, personal financial goals, and business planning objectives are aligned.

- Work with a professional to get a snapshot of your financial condition (including key components like assets, cash flow, and estate planning).

- Make sure all assets are optimized based on your own unique risk tolerance (defined as the degree of negative change that an investor can handle in the value of his portfolio).

- Measure your success, and make adjustments when appropriate.

- Control business and household expenses by tracking the last twelve months' expenses and by setting a budget going forward.

- Provide for an appropriate level of reserves to launch your business and to sustain some of the market swings and seasonality

Once an agent has experienced success in the industry, and starts to bring in a reasonable level of discretionary income, exploring appropriate retirement plans andother strategies to defer or reduce taxes becomes critical.

Once you've tackled the big-picture items, you'll want to drill down on a few key financial planning points. If you decide to work effectively with a financial planner, this person will probably go over each of these components. If you're doing it on your own, here's a look at the various aspects of your personal and business life that should be addressed in order to create a complete plan:

- Cash flow
- Investment planning
- Tax strategies
- Retirement planning
- Retirement distribution
- Current situation, risk tolerance, time horizon, and personal and financial goals
- Estate planning (or for high-net-worth individuals, wealth preservation)
- Education planning
- Risk management (death, disability, long-term care)
- Special needs (disabilities, senior dependen

- Survivorship

- Educational needs

- Business succession and continuity

- Immediate cash needs (reserves)

Other Considerations

Regardless of what path you take in creating a long-term plan for your business and life, there are a few key elements that you won't want to neglect. In addition to those already discussed, here are a few other building blocks that you'll want to take into consideration when working on your own plan:

- Health Insurance: These days, health insurance is a big concern for everyone—particularly for smallbusiness owners. No one appears to have completely overcome this, except to line up with some type of employer that offers lifetime benefits, or project higher-than-average cost increases to pay the premiums. Unless they're fortunate enough to have a spouse with a full-time job and benefits, most real estate agents grapple with the issue of health insurance coverage at some point during their career. Joining them in the struggle are a large number of self-employed professionals who—particularly in recent years, have found themselves shut out of the affordable health insurance market.

The Long-Term View

There's no time like the present to take a long-term view of your real estate career and create a plan for developing your business and providing a stable future for yourself and your family. Getting there requires a well-rounded view of your own finances and your financial goals, and a measurement of what kind of risk you're willing to take to get there. Here are some examples for various stages of the business:

• New Real Estate Agent: A real estate agent who is new in the business lacks the financial means and wherewithal to create a complete financial plan, but that doesn't mean he or she can't:

  ➢ Shell out a small fee to start a SEP-IRA plan for the future.

  ➢ Shop around for a good health insurance plan.

  ➢ Purchase a term life insurance policy.

- Agent with Two Years of Experience: An agent with two years under his belt and a child who is six years away from college will want to take all of the steps mentioned above, plus:

➤ Start a 529 or other college savings plan.

➤ Sit down with a financial planner to incorporate more elements into a long-term plan for personal financial success.

➤ Consider a retirement plan that allows for larger contributions (such as a 401(k) plan).

➤ Factor in other issues like long-term care and investment accounts (such as mutual funds or individual stocks).

➤ Think about investing in real estate as part of his overall investment portfolio.

- Agent with Ten Years of Experience: Depending on the agent's financial situation, and just how much planning done along the way, this agent will want to take all of the steps outlined above.

CHAPTER SEVEN

Be Available For Your Clients

Be Available and Maximizing Your Time

- Developing a service plan

The best way to provide the level of service you and your client agree upon is to create two checklists, a New Listing Checklist that details the steps you will follow when accepting a listing and a Sale Agreement Checklist that details all the steps that happen from contract to close. Standard procedures vary from state to state and MLS board to MLS board.

Ask the agents in your office what extra touches work for them.

The most significant challenge in an entrepreneurial business like real estate sales is managing time effectively. The daily battle against pro- crastination, distractions, interruptions, low-priority activities, and ingrained client expectations of instant accessibility can exhaust even the most energetic agent and can derail the plans of all but the most disciplined time manager.

This chapter helps you take control of your calendar, giving you the time you need to build skills, prospect, follow up with leads, plan and make quality pre- sentations, market properties, and position and present yourself successfully. Your ability to manage your days and invest your time for the highest return will separate you from the other agents who are vying for top-producer status and also enable you to earn your desired income.

- Spending Less Time to Accomplish More

Many real estate agents invest too much time and too little urgency in their businesses. They commit well over 40 hours to the job, and they put them- selves on call seven days a week. They spread themselves thin, and then, in order to sustain themselves over this endless schedule, they dilute their intensity. No other professional works so many hours. Even doctors have a lighter on-call schedule than most agents choose to accept. This is even truer in today's technology-based world of instant communication.

A real estate agent lives in an over-stimulated world. The sensory overload of smartphones, emails, text messages, websites, and social media makes the time-management challenges more acute than ever.

I suggest that you commit right now to become more effective in way less time each week. Consider this advice:

Set aside at least one day a week to recharge and refresh yourself. Before you say you can't afford the day off, realize this truth: Work expands to fill the time you give it. Reduce your work hours and you'll automatically squeeze more productivity into shorter spans of time. The day off should be a true day off. That means you shut down access (your smartphone, email, social media, and so on) and enjoy your family and other activities without interruption.

Increase your productivity by increasing your intensity. Give yourself deadlines with no procrastination options. If you know you need to accomplish a lineup of goals over the course of a five-day workweek, your focus automatically zooms in, you sweep away distractions, and you get the job done in the time allowed. I watched my own focus and productivity intensify as I went from a seven-day workweek to a six-day workweek to a five-day workweek. The largest production increase I experienced, though, was when I moved to a schedule of four days of work followed by three days off, with no correlating reduction in my income or success objectives. Given my goals, I knew I had to work with incredibly high intensity and no options for procrastination.

Take away your time-wasting options. Commit to time off and force yourself to work during established, reasonable work hours. Automatically, you'll force yourself to eliminate time-wasting activities.

Give yourself no option to add hours back to your workweek. If you allow yourself the option to add time back to your workweek, you leave yourself open to time-wasting choices. Begin to treat time as your most valuable asset. Real estate agents are too casual with their time, leading to career, relationship, or bank-account casu- alties that could be avoided by treating time as life's most precious resource.

Applying Pareto's Principle: The 80:20 Rule

In the late 1800s, an Italian economist named Vilfredo Pareto observed that in Italy a small group of people held nearly all the power, influence, and money, which they used to create a significant advantage over the rest of the popu- lation. He theorized that in most countries about 80 percent of the wealth

and power was controlled by about 20 percent of the people. He called this a "predictable imbalance," which eventually became known as the 80:20 rule.

In the 1900s, researchers realized that the theory of a "vital few and trivial many" — 20 percent of the participants accounting for 80 percent of the results — applies across many fields of expertise. Most certainly, it's true when it comes to time investment, and here's what that means to you:

Eighty percent of your results are generated by 20 percent of your hard- fought efforts. Conversely, 20 percent of your results are generated by 80 percent of your mediocre efforts. In other words, one-fifth of your time-consuming activities delivers four-fifths of your gross sales or gross commissions.

You can increase the productivity that results from your time investment by assessing which activities achieve the highest-quality results. Too many agents allow their time to be consumed by activities that generate a mere 20 percent of their revenue. The moment they shift their time investment into higher-return activities, they see dramatic income results.

The 80:20 rule holds true across a spectrum of life activities. Whether you're investing in your career, relationships, health, wealth, or personal develop- ment, 20 percent of your efforts deliver 80 percent of the results you seek. The secret is to figure out which activities deliver the highest-quality returns and invest your time accordingly.

Do you make time for the few activities that return the most significant results? Or are you, like most people in the world, giving your time to the time-gobbling 80 percent of activities that deliver a meager return?

Top performers in nearly any field quickly identify which actions account for the great majority of results, and they weight their time toward those activi- ties, performing them with great regularity and intensity.

Following is the list of the half-dozen important activities that I share with all of my real estate coaching clients:

1. Prospecting

2. Lead follow up

3. Listing presentations

4. Buyer interview presentations

5. Showing property to qualified buyers

6. Writing and negotiating contracts

If you dedicate yourself to these six activities, you'll see high returns on your time investment. Flip the principle to your advantage. Begin spending more and more of your time on the activities that are proven to deliver results, and refuse to be crushed by the weight and waste of those that don't.

Making time for the things that impact your success

If controlling time and gaining discipline to invest hours in better, higher- value activities were easy, everyone would be making big money in real estate sales. Facts prove otherwise.

On average, newer agents make less than $20,000 a year. Almost certainly the low-income statistics correlate with poor time-allocation choices.

To allocate larger amounts of time to success-generating actions, follow what I call the four Ds:

1. Decide that your time-management skills, habits, and activities are going to change.

This is a challenging first step for most people. That's because changing behavior isn't easy, and time usage is a behavior. To avoid change, people search for solutions that enable them to keep doing what they've always done. In doing so, they waste yet more time by vacillating between the change they know they must face and the hope that they won't have to face it.

I believe that the biggest waste of time occurs from the moment you know you need to do something and when you actually set out to do it. That's why it's so important to make an immediate commitment to change your time-management patterns and habits. Make the decision to change today!

2. Define what needs to change. This step involves two phases. First you have to determine the specific activities that are causing you to waste time or sacrifice productivity. Then you have to figure out how you can remedy the situation.

For example, do you need to get to your office earlier each day? Does that mean you need to go to sleep earlier each night? Do you need more prospecting time or more time for lead follow up? Does that mean you need to turn off your cellphone to minimize distractions when you're trying to undertake these activities?

What is barring your success?

I worked with a client a few years ago who had difficulty getting into the office early enough to begin his day. We tracked it back to the fact that he was going to bed too late to be able to reach his office consistently by 8 a.m. when he needed his day to start.

We further determined that he needed a certain amount of time in the evening to have dinner with his family, play with his children, put them to bed, and then have time with his wife before their bedtime. He needed to be home from work by a certain hour for all of this to happen effi- ciently and consistently for him.

After he made the necessary changes, by coming in earlier and leaving the office on time, his income shot up dramatically. The quality of life with his children and wife skyrocketed, as well, all the result of defining the problem, designing a solution, and managing time accordingly.

3. Design a time-management plan. Get proactive rather than reactive.

Typical day planners and smartphone scheduling apps are reactionary time-management tools. They enable you to schedule time for client needs, appointments, and limited activities, but they don't help you take control of time for your own priorities and purposes. You need to do that part on your own.

To master your time, you need to adopt a time-blocking system that dedicate predetermined periods of time to your most valuable activities. The upcoming section describes time blocking in detail. The key point is that you can't leave your days vulnerable to the time needs of others. You must block out periods of time for your own priority activities. Otherwise, you risk giving your days away to the appointment or time requests of clients and colleagues, leaving yourself no time for your own needs. No wonder so many agents feel like they're being pulled like taffy.

4. Just do it!

Don't wait to analyze every aspect of every problem and design the absolutely perfect solution before taking action. Waiting promises only unrealized income, unfulfilled potential, and limited wealth. Instead, decide what to change, define how to change, design a time-management plan that allows for change, and then just do it.

Weighting your time to what matters

In order to achieve success, any newer agent must commit a minimum of 15 hours a week to DIPA, or direct income-producing activities. That means that you need to dedicate 15 hours every single week — three hours every day — to prospecting and lead follow up. Do that, and you assure your success and income. Fail to do so and your success is in question.

Don't cheat by trying to replace DIPA tasks with what I call IIPA, or indirect income-producing activities. IIPA tasks include things like making client- development marketing pieces, producing direct mailings, creating or fiddling with your website, optimizing your search-engine placement, publishing news- letters, and a near-endless list of other efforts that agents invest in to indi- rectly produce income.

All social media is IIPA. Yes, you read that correctly. Although social media is valuable to your business, the truth is that far too many agents expect social media to replace all other forms of lead generation. Too often agents think they can sit behind their computers and generate large volumes of quality leads.

Social media is a wonderful way to communicate with, engage, and listen to clients, past clients, and prospects. But balancing your time is essential. You can spend hours checking posts and private messages, but you're faking yourself out if you think that's a productive use of your time. The key is to invest just 30 to 60 minutes a day in social media.

The problem is, IIPA activities are difficult to control in terms of the time, effort, energy, and dollars they require, and they're almost impossible to measure in terms of outcome. Often, countless hours of your work result in marketing pieces that go straight to the trash bin, emails that are deleted with a single keystroke, or social-media posts that don't reach the right audience.

Indirect marketing efforts result in a high quantity of contacts. Direct market ing efforts result in high-quality contacts and sales success is the result of quality rather than quantity.

Aim to spread your time between DIPA and IIPA tasks on at least a four-to- one ratio: For every hour you spend in IIPA, spend at least four hours in DIPA. Veer from that ratio and you risk dramatic income swings rather than consistent revenue growth.

Keeping PSA time in check
Agents spend an undue amount of time on production-supporting activities, or PSAs. These activities include all the steps necessary to support such direct income-producing activities as prospecting, following up on leads, taking listings,

and making sales. You can't avoid the administrative functions that support your sales and client-service efforts, but you can and should handle them in the fewest number of hours possible.

- Using your time wisely

PSA functions surrounding sales tend to be recurring, requiring weekly or even daily attention. Here are several ways to keep these supporting tasks on a firm leash:

- Streamline the process.

Determine whether you can create a system to make it faster, possibly eliminating some unnecessary steps. Instead of doing it once for each prospect, can you do several at once, batching the work for greater efficiency? It takes almost as much time to assemble one set of marketing-material packages and brochures as it does ten. Invest the time to create the ten and have nine ready to go out the door.

- Create templates.

Don't craft a sales or lead follow-up letter from scratch each time. The same goes for proposals. You can take a basic format and customize it for individual use.

- Batch your work.

Make your PSA calls one after another. Bunch together the PSA actions as much as possible so you can move quickly from one similar call or action to another.

- Eliminate the step.

Sometimes your examination of process may uncover that a particular function doesn't need to be done at all.

- Delegate.

Is there administrative help somewhere in your sales department? Can you find someone to lend a hand? Are there internship pro- grams that might provide some eager business students who want to learn the business from the ground up? A talk with your sales manager may help.

Hire help

If you can't get support within your department, are you willing to pay a few bucks for it? Maybe you can hire a college or high- school student, a stay-at-home parent, or a part-timer who just wants a low-pressure opportunity to earn a little money. For many of the PSA tasks that aren't proprietary, the work can be done off-site.

Asking for referrals to turn PSA into DIPA

When you must turn to PSA work, you can often take the opportunity to get in a little DIPA action at the same time. For instance, client-service follow-up calls are part of your production-supporting activities. Checking to confirm that the prospect or client has received expected materials or information is a routine task that doesn't relate directly to income generation.

But don't stop there, get some extra mileage from this PSA effort by turning your client service call into a prospecting call: Ask for a referral.

It's never too early in a sales relationship to begin building a referral base. A truly qualified referral request, however, takes a little time and attention. Be ready to invest at least five minutes in conversation to avoid appearing like a hit-and-run referral driver. You may use a great segue statement like:

"I have a very important question to ask you."

This statement forces a pause, builds anticipation, and sets the tone for a meaningful conversation. And it requests permission to explore client or prospect contacts. You may use a script like this to help you:

"I'm delighted that I've been able to serve you. I was wondering about others you might know who would also benefit from my service. Could we explore for a few minutes other individuals you believe I might be able to serve?"

Managing Your Day

How often do you exclaim at the end of the day, "Where did the day go?" It's as if we've gotten nothing of significance done in the last eight hours on the job. When you feel that way, go back and review the mix of PSA, IIPA, and DIPA. How much time was spent in each category?

If you find that your time investment was a little off-balance, accept that today is gone, but tomorrow can be a new opportunity to get it right. Spend a few minutes figuring out where the day did go. Did you put off tackling your DIPA tasks until your day was derailed by interruptions? Were you so engrossed in IIPA tracking that you spent more time than you intended in analyzing the results? Did you lose momentum by jumping back and forth between prospecting and lead follow up?

Pinpoint the problems, plan for the next day, and nail down a schedule that ensures maximum productivity and keeps you on the path toward success.

The power of the 11 a.m. rule

The 11 a.m. rule goes like this: The world around a real estate agent gears up at 11 each morning. Attorneys, title officers, loan officers, other agents, appraisers, home inspectors, repair contractors, and clients will most likely call you after or close to 11 a.m.

Because of this, it's imperative that you come into the office early and complete your prospecting and lead follow up before the clock strikes the hour.

I even suggest the extreme approach of not answering your phone until 11 in order to minimize the chance of being distracted during your most important production hours.

Tracking your time

It's hard to know exactly how much time you spend on DIPA, IIPA, and PSA functions unless you've tracked your activities over a period of time to deter- mine an average. This is very important, and it supports an undeniable truth in sales: When performance is measured, performance improves. By tracking your time usage, you're guaranteed to increase your time effectiveness.

Here's how this form can help you make the most of those increments:

Keep the form with you and fill it out as you go. Don't wait until the end of the day to complete it, you're bound to forget something.

Track yourself for at least a week, longer is better. This allows for daily anomalies and helps create more of an "average" work flow.

Dealing with time-consuming fires

Time-consuming fires are the hot issues that result from the emotional turmoil involved in many real estate transactions. Sometimes they require calm and caution; other times you need to put on a fireman's hat and start dousing the flames of a delayed closing; emotionally frustrated buyer or seller; problem co-op agent; or slow-moving inspector, appraiser, or loan officer. Let the following rules guide your responses:

Rule #1: There is no closing issue that can't wait an hour. When your transaction hits a snag, don't let it dramatically change your day's schedule. Wait to resolve the issue during the time you've blocked for administrative tasks.

Rule #2: A frenzied reaction only adds fuel to the fire. More often than not, when one closing party gets riled it's because someone else in the transaction is riled and hysteria is catching. Aim to serve as the calming influence in the transaction. If the problem arises two hours before your predetermined administrative time slot, inform the parties that you have prescheduled appointments that you can't change, but that you'll be able to take action when you get out of the appointments in two hours.

Rule #3: Fires often burn themselves out. Rather than jump into the mess, give the issue a bit of time to simmer down. Remember that your prospecting and lead follow-up tasks are appointments to which you've committed. Sticking with your daily plan may give the issue time to cool or even resolve itself.

Rule #4: Don't wait for a three-alarm fire to call for the pump truck. If the fire becomes hot, suit up your broker right away. Before the transac- tion flares out of control, ask for help. The longer you delay, the more effort you'll spend getting the situation cooled down.

Time Blocking Your Way to Success

A time-blocked schedule reserves and protects slotted time segments for pre-planned, pre-determined activities. The objective of time blocking is to increase the amount of time you can invest in direct income-producing efforts.

Many people have heard of time blocking, but few master its use. The challenge isn't in creating the schedule; that's the easy part. The challenge is keeping on the schedule. That's the hard part, because most people set their time-blocking expectations very high, reserve large portions of time, and then can't maintain the schedule. The good news, though, is that even if you need to compromise your time blocks, you still come out ahead.

One of my coaching clients increased the number of units she sold by more than 100 in one year, at the same time increasing her sales volume by more than $17 million. Pretty amazing performance. I asked her how much of her time she spent on her ideal time-blocking schedule. Her answer: "About 50 percent of the time." She is proof that even maintaining half of your blocked- out time can produce incredible results.

Setting your schedule in time blocks

Good time blocking starts with a schedule grid. In the beginning, create a grid that breaks your schedule down into 30-minute segments. As your skill progresses, you may shift to a 15-minute grid format. As you complete the grid, I strongly suggest that you block your entire daily schedule, not just your workday. Follow these steps:

Block time for your personal life first. If you don't, you'll be hard pressed to squeeze in personal time after scheduling everything else. Decide which are the most important personal activities in your life and block them out before you allow any other obligations onto your calendar. Set aside a date night with your spouse or significant other. Block time for exercise, quiet time, prayer time, personal-development time, and family time.

Decide which full day you'll take off each week. You must take at least one day off. The reaction of new agents is, "Oh! I couldn't do that." Give me a break; even God took the seventh day off.

A few words on the definition of a day off: It means no real estate calls, no answering your cellphone, no negotiating offers, no taking ad calls, no taking sign calls, and no meeting with clients or prospects. The minute you do any business activity, it's a workday, even if it's just for five minutes. Honor yourself and your family with one day a week away from real estate. The 24/7 approach leads to family frustrations and burnout. It's hard to receive the love you need from a pile of money.

Decide which evenings you will and won't work. Again, set boundaries. I suggest that you make no more than three or four nights a week available to clients. Designate them during the time-blocking stage and then move prospects only into those evening time slots. I limited my own evening work to Tuesdays only. Every other night of the week my better half could expect me home no later than 6:30 for dinner if I had a 5:15 listing appointment.

Begin blocking time for DIPA, or direct income-producing activities. Block time for prospecting and lead follow up first, and preferably early in the day. I know what you're thinking: "Aren't more people home in the afternoon and evening?" Probably so. But will you prospect consistently if you do it in the evening? After more than two decades in real estate, I know for a fact that the answer is no. The fact that more people are home at night doesn't matter if that's not when you're picking up the phone to call them. Schedule calls for morning hours when you can and will make the contacts.

- Schedule time slots for appointments next. Determine how many appointments you need to hold and how long they need to run. How long do you need for a listing presentation? How much time do you need to show a buyer homes in a specific area?

- Schedule time for administrative tasks. This includes phone calls, office meetings, company property tours, and the like. Make a list of your regular, necessary activities and then put them into your time-blocked schedule.

Finally, block some flextime. Flextime helps you stay on track. It allows you to put out fires, make emergency calls, handle unscheduled but nec- essary tasks, and still stay on your schedule.

Most agents who are new to time blocking create schedules that are too rigid. The lack of flexibility causes them to be off their schedules before 10:30 in the morning. From that point, they're off schedule for the rest of the day.

As you start out, block about thirty minutes of flextime for every two hours of scheduled time in your daily grid. You can always reduce or remove the flextime blocks as your skills and discipline increase.

Avoiding time-blocking mistakes

Sales professionals in the top 10 percent of their industries share a common trait: They control, use, and invest their time more wisely and effectively than their lower-performing associates. Among sales professionals, time usage determines income.

The most significant challenge for most sales professionals is time control. Through years of study and coaching sales professionals, I've compiled the following list of challenges that most salespeople experience when trying to master their time-block schedule.

Mistake #1: Making yourself too available. The biggest error that salespeople make is getting sucked into the interruption game. You need times in your schedule that are free of interruptions, during which you bar access to all but those to whom you grant exceptions. Follow this advice:

Use an effective gatekeeper to screen your calls, redirecting all minor issues, problems, challenges, and interruptions that can be handled by an assistant or some other person.

Use your voicemail to screen and inform. Record a new voicemail greeting daily. Tell the listener when you're in appointments and when you'll be returning calls. This sets the standard that you're busy and valuable but also available.

Limit the number of people who have unfiltered access to you. Create a short list of the important few people who can interrupt your schedule at any time of the day, and don't let anyone else in during time blocked for interruption-free activities. As you make your own list, include only those who are extremely important to your personal life. Very few clients find their way onto the short lists of truly successful people.

Mistake #2: Choosing the wrong office location and set up. The nature of your physical office has a dramatic effect on your time management and productivity. Give serious consideration to the following two issues:

See that the size of your work environment matches the size of your practice. If you don't have enough square footage for yourself and your staff, your production will be stunted.

Don't let your physical space limit your growth opportunities. If you're crowded by your staff, you're in the wrong physical location.

Your personal office must be private. Top-producing agents have too many focused activities to be in the bullpen of activity. If you're surrounded by the buzz of the staff, inbound phone calls, problems, and challenges, it's too easy to be tempted to jump in and help, tackling the issues of servicing at the expense of new business creation. The only way to control your planning and pros- pecting environment is to locate your practice in a private office away from distractions and staff.

Mistake #3: Failing to operate on an appointment-only basis. Too many agents are willing to meet at all hours of the day and night and on a moment's notice. By time blocking, you can create appointment slots and drive prospects into those slots, just as your doctor, dentist, or attorney does.

Studies show that 80 percent of all prospects are willing to fit into the schedules of their professional advisors. But when they aren't alerted to a schedule, they take control on their own, dictating the appointment time and leaving an agent like you juggling your schedule to adapt to their needs. Realtors accept this knee-jerk scheduling approach as a necessary aspect of a "service-oriented" business, as if total availability equals service.

Operate as a professional on an appointment-only basis, with all appointments scheduled during time-blocked periods when you know you'll be available, focused, and uninterrupted by any issue other than the one your client is sharing.

Mistake #4: Bowing to distractions. Real estate sales is among the most interrupted and distracted professions on the face of the planet. Realtors are distracted by the constant jangle of desk phones, home phones, and cellphones.

If the phone isn't ringing, you have the distraction of email, usually inter- rupting you with some unsolicited miracle offer or, less often, with a new lead opportunity. Here's a tip: Don't derail your day just because your computer tells you that you've got mail. Control distractions following this advice:

Block time in your day for the distractions you know you'll encoun- ter. If you want to socialize with other agents, plan a set time to do that. Just remember to keep it short and limit the coffee klatch to the time you allocated for it.

Create a list of no more than five people who are granted instant access during your workday. Have your assistant memorize the names. If you don't have an assistant, work with your receptionist so that only those few people are granted unfiltered access.

Position yourself as an agent-in-command versus an agent-on-demand. Block your time and maintain your schedule. Rather than putting yourself at the beck and call of others during all hours of the day and night, work on an appointment basis, eliminate distractions, and take control of your days, your business, your income, and your life.

Killing the Time Killer Called Procrastination

The number-one obstacle between real estate agents and higher production is interruptions. A close second is procrastination.

Procrastination is the direct result of a lack of urgency to do what needs to be done and to do it now. Urgency is directly linked to success. You can increase your output by 30 percent if you work with urgency in mind.

It's based on the premise that you'll never have enough time to do everything you want or need to do, but that in every day you'll always have enough time to accomplish the most important tasks. Obviously, you won't get to the most important tasks if you're bogged down with tasks of low importance that can easily wait until later. Nor will you get to the most important tasks if you procrastinate.

An upcoming section in this chapter helps you set priorities. After you set your priorities, take action without procrastination by following these two pieces of advice:

Limit the time in which you can get the job done. Too much time to work can lower urgency and lead to procrastination. By identifying days off and time off, you raise the efficiency and effectiveness of your produc- tion on the days you're working.

Give yourself deadlines. Have you ever noticed how much gets done when you're leaving on vacation in a day or so? I've seen people double or triple their work output in the days leading up to a vacation. What if you operated every day at that pace and urgency? Your income and quality of life would explode to heights you never imagined.

Moving forward with a clear vision

A good deal of procrastination results directly from the lack of a clear vision or clarity about what to do. If you don't know what you want, you can't possibly achieve it. You can hardly hit a target you can't see. Clarity of purpose kills procrastination, yet fewer than 3 percent of all people define and write down their goals.

Answer these questions:

What do you want to be?

What do you want to do with your life?

What do you want to have?

Where do you want to go?

I know you want to be financially independent. Otherwise, you wouldn't be in real estate sales. But what does financial independence mean to you? How much money do you need to live the lifestyle you dream about? The famous success motivator Napoleon Hill explains the importance of identifying your goal when he says, "There is one quality that one must possess to win, and that is definiteness of purpose, the knowledge of what one wants and a burning desire to achieve it."

- Clarify your desires.

When you're certain about what you want to achieve, you'll find it far easier to set and follow an action plan that isn't hindered by the problem of procrastination.

- Knowing your objectives

You'll set annual goals, of course. But also view each day that you work or play in terms of daily objectives. What do you want to accomplish today? What result do you want to effect by day's end?

- Setting your priorities

Your priorities are the most important actions or steps you must take in order to achieve your objectives for the day. Objectives and priorities aren't one and the same. Objectives are results you intend to achieve. Priorities are steps you take to achieve success.

By prioritizing the importance or value of the tasks on your to-do list, you greatly increase the probability that you'll be motivated to overcome procrastination and get the job done.

Most people go about creating task lists in the wrong way. They write down all of the things they must do each day and then go to work, proudly ticking off items as they are completed and equating their level of success with the number of items they check off the list. Success, though, doesn't result from how many things you get done. It results from getting the right things done. In other words, you need to know your priorities.

Following is an outline for the prioritization system I've used with success for years:

1. Create your daily task list as you normally would. Don't think at all about what is most important. Just think about what needs to get done over the course of the day. Put yourself in brainstorming mode and get your thoughts down on paper.

2. When you have your list, create task categories. You're not prioritizing during this step. This isn't about what to do first, second, or third. All you're doing is sorting tasks into these categories:

A. You'll suffer a significant consequence if you don't complete these tasks today. If it means you have to work all day and all night, these items must get done.

B. These tasks trigger a mild consequence if they aren't completed today. You probably wouldn't stay late to finish them.

C. These tasks have no penalty at all if they aren't done today.

D. These tasks can be delegated. They involve low-value activities that should be performed by someone who has a lower hourly dollar value than you.

E. These tasks can and should be eliminated. They probably made their way onto your list out of tradition or habit. They aren't neces- sary, so you need to figure out a way to get them off the list. I call it pruning.

3. When your list is categorized, prioritize the tasks. Begin with your A category and determine which item deserves A-1 status. Follow by desig- nating A-2, A-3, A-4, A-5, and so on. Then repeat the process for the B, C, and D categories. Go to work in the order of these priorities, and you'll be amazed at how you can accomplish more in less time without falling into the procrastination trap.

As you master the art of prioritizing, expect to see fewer cross-offs or check- marks on your task list. By undertaking your most important tasks first, you'll complete fewer but more important activities.

Consider every day that you achieve closure on all your A category items a terrific success. If you complete your A items on every single one of the days you work this year, I guarantee that you'll see your production and income explode.

Giving yourself deadlines and rewards

It's human instinct to move away from pain and toward the pleasures of life. That's why you have to link deadlines with rewards if you want to keep your self motivated to complete your work in a sustained way. Without a reward, it's darned hard to face the rigor of a difficult task. Each day when you set your objectives and priorities, set deadlines as well. Then link completion of your tasks with a clearly defined reward.

For example, set a deadline to get all of your prospecting and lead follow-up calls done by 10:30 a.m., and then reward yourself with a trip to your favorite coffee shop or lunch restaurant. Beyond that, promise yourself that if you meet your deadlines and complete all of your priorities for a full week, you'll reward yourself with a massage, facial, or special evening out.

Realize these two truths about rewards:

You have to give them to yourself. Don't expect to receive them from your broker, clients, prospects, staff, or even family.

You have to set interim goals to keep you moving forward on a consis- tent basis. If your reward is financial independence, your payoff may not arrive for 10 or 20 years. That's way too long to wait for a pat on the back.

Sales involves high pay, for sure, but also a fair amount of rejection and dis- couragement in between. Rewards encourage you to do the things you know you should do even when you don't feel like doing them.

Handle intrusive clients

In real estate, we're in a client-service business. We place a high level of value on our clients. But the thought of "the client is always right" can be taken too far.

You know that in order to provide the best service to each client, you have to seek some balance. If the "squeaky-wheel" clients take up more than their share of your time and resources, you won't be able to give the atten- tion to other deserving clients.

It's important to educate clients about your availability. Let new custom- ers know your schedule and the best times to reach you, as well as how to leave a message when you can't be reached. As part of this education, you also want to establish how quickly they can expect a response from you after they leave a message: 24 hours? The same business day?

As for existing clients and clients, be sure to update them whenever your availability circumstances change. If you make changes to your schedule, notify them of the schedule revisions and your new availability. Depending upon the importance of the client and the immediacy of the situations you deal with, you may even want to let clients know when you're on vacation or on a business trip so they know your response time will be longer.

Creating reasonable expectations is key in good client relations. It may not be unreasonable to take 24 hours to return a client's call, but not if the client is used to and expects to hear from you within an hour.

You can also reinforce this through your voicemail message. When you leave your availability and response details as part of your message, callers are more likely to recall and retain.

Don't be tempted to include, as many agents do, "If it's an emergency, call me on my cellphone," unless you're prepared for lots of interruptions. After all, isn't interruption exactly what you're trying to avoid?

Keep phone calls short

Especially when you're making or taking transaction-servicing calls or production-support calls, you need to conduct business in the shortest time period possible. Otherwise you'll erode the time you need for high-value income-producing activities. To keep calls short, employ these techniques:

Establish an indication of the time available as you begin the call. For example, say something like, "I have an appointment in 15 minutes, but your call was an important one, and I wanted to get back to you as quickly as I could." This technique alerts the call recipient to your time limitation. It says, nicely, "Get to the point quickly." It underscores that you value the caller and made a special effort to make time for the conversation. If you're on a time-blocked schedule, everything is treated as an appoint- ment, including times for returning phone calls, so you'll be speaking the truth. You do have another appointment in 15 minutes. This technique is particularly appropriate for prospect or client calls.

Offer an alternative to a short phone call. If you think your client or prospect wants or needs more than a short return phone call, follow the above technique but then go one step further: Assure the other person that 15 minutes should be more than enough time, but if it's not you can schedule a phone conference when you'll be available for an appoint- ment later in the day. I've made this offer many times, and I've never had to talk with the client later. We've always managed to resolve the issues during the short conversation.

When possible, handle production-support calls with voicemail mes- sages. You don't want to rely on voicemail with prospects, because you want to establish personal relationships that lead to face-to-face meet- ings. But when you're handling service calls, voicemail is a time-effective option for both you and the other party. Make a call, leave a message, and offer the option to call you back with the assurance that if your mes- sage resolves the issue then there is no need for a return call. Follow a script such as this one:

"Jack, I know that you're busy. I believe that this resolves the issue. If you agree, there is no need for you to call me back. If you do need to speak with me, I'll be available later today between 3:30 and 4:15. Please call me then."

CHAPTER EIGHT

Problem Solving

Mindset and Action

In TheTraveler's Gift, Andy Andrews passes on the wisdom that "our lives are fashioned by choice. First we make choices. Then our choices make us." I wholeheartedly agree. We are what we decide we will be, and we do what we decide we will do. We become our choices.The twelve issues you face in a shifting marketare really an opportunity.An opportunity to make the twelve most important choices that will directly impact your career and power you through any shift. Of these twelve choices the first and most significant will be to get real about your situation and get right about what you're doing.

When a shift occurs confusion follows. Not only in the marketplace but also in the mind and body. What to think and what to do becomes fuzzy because what once worked is no longer working and you may not know why. Don't let yourself panic. Keep fear at bay. When a market shifts there is only one thing to do—shift with it. In truth, there are two shifts you must make. A mental shift and an action shift.

The Mental Shift

I believe that your life will be either about your problems or your opportunities. You'll either be running away from something or running towards something. It's your call. To survive a shift you must first make the mental shift to run towards what you most want and avoid the temptation of running away from what you most fear. One approach lifts you up and the other drags you down. You must keep both eyes on your target and not the ever-moving market. Remember that success is never about the chosen few, but always about the few who choose. You get to choose and your life builds from there.

There are three types of people who emerge when a market shifts. First, those that fearfully predict the worst and are unnecessarily pessi- mistic; second, those who hopefully wish for the best, believe they can't fail and are unrealistically positive; and, third, those who respect the fact that they might fail, actively prepare for the worst and strive for the best. These are the resourcefully realistic and are always the time- ly triumphant. They are matter-of-fact about the market and sensible about their situation. They see things as they are and openly acknowl- edge how they're doing. At the same time they stay optimistic about their opportunities. As my friend Zig Ziglar says "they do a checkup from the neck up" and make sure that even though the market is re- shaping itself it isn't reshaping their attitude.

You can't control the market but you can control your outlook and your response to the market. Remain resolute. Know that while every- one won't succeed in a shift, some will and anyone can. You must be an "anyone can." This is not just a short-term attitude you adopt, but a life- long posture you take. It's a journey you embark on led by the mental choices you make. Be certain of this—your mindset matters.

Most people lead a "flow with the tides" life. Their careers and their fortunes seem to rise and fall with the tides of the market. When things are going well anything and everything works— their boats float. What they fail to realize is that literally all boats float at high tide and no captain gets credit for that! When times get tough and the tide goes out, all of a sudden not everything works. Their boats don't float. Those quick to adjust will have a floating boat. On the rocks or out at sea, the choice is yours.

Be a low-tider always be prepared for low tide. Know that it is al- ways a good time to be in the real estate market when you take a long-term view of the market instead of getting caught up in its short-term volatility. Know that there is always enough business for you to survive with a minimum income while striving for your maximum. Keep your perspective. Judge your success over the length of your career not the high or low of any single year. Know that growth comes from clarity, priorities and focused-action. The first two are how you think and the last is what you do. To make a strong mental shift be clear about your situation and what it is you want. Write down and prioritize the necessary steps you must take to achieve your goals. Now you're focused on what you want, you know what you need to do, and you know what comes first. So what are you waiting for?

The Action Shift

Once you've gotten real, you've got to get right—right into action and into the right action. For all the necessity of knowing what to do, taking the right action now is just as necessary. Once you know then it's not about more knowing—it's about doing. The difference between a career worth having and a career worth heaving is the amount of focused ac- tion you take every day. It's about knowing what to do and then doing it. Keller Williams CEO Mark Willis often shares that his inspirational and energetic mother, Rachael Willis, always taught him to "Do right—Fear not." When you do the right things you leave fear behind.

When you know what to do it's time to move from inspiration to perspiration. So the straightforward question that jumps right at you in a shift is a simple one. "What do I do right now?" Actually, this is a two-part question that first asks "what must be done right?" and then "what must be done now?" The answer to that two-part question becomes your focus and yours alone. Understand what worked yesterday probably won't work today and what matters now probably didn't then. When the market shifts, new strate- gies are required and new actions are critical.

In a shifted market there is little room for mistakes and that is a real challenge. The margin for error is very thin. Where there was once latitude, there isn't. You must be focused on the right tasks and you must execute them well. Efficiency and effectiveness are essential contribu- tors to your bottom line.One way to look at the necessary actions is by roles, yours and oth- ers. The challenge you might have is that you thought there were some roles you had delegated to others only to discover that you hadn't done so successfully. The net result is that you must personally start doing certain tasks again. The critical actions that you identify must be carried out by you or personally overseen by you on a daily basis. Our research shows that the two actions real estate agents must take personal ownership of are lead generation and lead conversion. Nothing becomes more critical to success than finding motivated buyers and sellers and closing them to an appointment. Your active involvement in the lead conversion process gives you two invaluable gifts. First, you get an immediate and ongoing sense of the issues of the market—the buyer and seller objections that need to be overcome. Second, you will get an honest understanding of the conversion rates that are possible. No one on your team will be as talented or as invested in closing leads to appointments, and your direct participa- tion allows you to set the standard and coach your team on how they too can meet it. It's what I call "management by wandering around." But it's not really wandering. I want to periodically and regularly insert myself into critical areas of the business. Sam Walton made a habit of visiting all his stores and working cash registers for hours. His interaction with cus- tomers gave him vital insight into what was and was not working.

To put lead generation and lead conversion in less effective hands than yours could spell the difference between success and failure. Fail- ure is never an option. As business analysts have often pointed out, "the seeds of failure are usually sown during times of success." The most humbling lesson of a shift is this— we succeed in good times not only because of what we do right, but also in spite of what we do wrong.

The remaining eleven tactics involve making some of the most important choices you'll ever make and mastering some of the most important skills you'll ever master. What you did right in the past will be reevaluated and what you did wrong corrected. In each one, you will most likely have to ask, "Who should be doing this? Me or someone else?" The way to resolve this is by asking one more question: "Who will do this the best?" Don't fight the answer.

As you go through the list of necessary actions, don't be surprised if they're not special, unique, or new. Actually, they are the foundational components of any successful real estate career. Our research with the best agents in the industry for our book The Millionaire Real Estate Agent and our ongoing dialogues with them absolutely show that the top agents become top agents by mastering the fundamentals. Maybe the reason the basics are so often abandoned is the fact that they aren't special, unique, or new. When business gets tight, they reveal themselves as the timeless factors that determine the difference between success or failure. School is never out for the motivated. The basics are never outdated.

CHAPTER NINE

Get Leads Anyway You Can

Prospecting is one of the easiest but most misunderstood concepts in the field of real estate sales. This is especially true with the explosion of online lead generation. Attempting to balance prospecting and marketing has never been more difficult.

Sales trainers constantly try to sell their "prospecting-free systems" on worldwide speaking circuits, basically saying, "You'll never have to prospect again if you use my system." And because salespeople secretly don't want to prospect, they readily buy into the too-good-to-be-true no-prospecting philosophy. But both marketing and prospecting have a place in your business. The correct positioning is to be prospecting focused and marketing enhanced.

As a salesperson, if you buy into the myth of a prospecting-free or marketing- only system, you're failing to master sound prospecting approaches, and you're abandoning the need to continually develop new leads. You're risking your very livelihood in the real estate business. Prospecting is the pathway to sales success.

Knowing Why to Prospect

The purpose of prospecting is to develop prospective clients for your business. The real estate prospecting process involves two steps.

1. Identify and create leads by establishing contact with people who have interest in what you're offering and the ability to become clients of your business. Prospecting can be making connections with your friends and past clients and specifically asking for referrals. The key is the last statement, "specifically asking for referrals."

2. Secure a face-to-face appointment for a pre-determined time in the future.

Real estate agents seek two categories of clients: sellers, who become listing clients, and buyers, who become real estate purchasers. The following sections provide tips on how to prospect for clients in each group.

Prospecting for Sellers

Listing leads come from past clients, those in your sphere of influence, expired listings, FSBO conversions, open houses, notices of default, non-owner- occupied homes, lead cultivation, and door knocking, but they rarely come without some effort, and here's why. The tendency when people are sending you referrals is to send you prospective buyers. The public's perception is that real estate agents sell houses: that we put people in our cars and drive them around and find them a home to buy. If you evaluate thousands of agents' businesses, as I have, you'll see that most referrals are buyers.

To find sellers, you have to do some pretty active prospecting work:

Seller referrals don't come naturally. Specifically ask those within your sphere of influence, your circle of past clients, and your referral groups to share the names of people who need or want to sell real estate.

To achieve a greater listing inventory and develop a specialty as a listing agent, cultivate listing prospects by working expired and FSBO listings.

Prospecting for buyers

Prospecting for buyers is easier than prospecting for sellers, in part because referrals arrive more naturally and in part because open houses attract prospective buyers and provide you with such a great prospecting platform. Additionally, buyers are more naturally created from your marketing efforts. Most agents will have far more buyer opportunities than seller opportunities or leads.

If you're short on buyer prospects, increase the frequency of your open houses. The real estate industry has shifted to a more do-it-yourself buyer. According to NAR, 63 percent of prospective buyers have walked through a home they first viewed online. The vast majority use open houses because they don't have to reveal themselves as buyers and register their contact information. They get to remain stealth.

The types of houses you choose to show determine the kinds of prospects you generate. Obviously, higher-priced and more-exclusive properties draw more-discerning buyer prospects, and lower-priced properties attract less-affluent prospects.

To build your business quickly, work to generate leads from more first-time home buyers by planning more open houses in the low range of your marketplace. The benefits of developing first-time buyer prospects include

First-time buyers can be sold into homes quickly because they aren't burdened with the need to sell homes in order to make purchases possible. They lack experience with other real estate agents. They don't have current agent affiliations, nor do they approach a new real estate agent relationship with baggage that may have   been acquired from a less- than-stellar past experience.

They acquire strong loyalty when good service is rendered, allowing you to establish a long-term relationship that may span 10 to 15 years and multiple home sales and purchases during that period.

They   provide you with an opportunity to establish relationships with their friends who are also considering first-time purchases.

Understanding the Four Pillars of Prospecting

For long-term prospecting success, apply these four disciplines that are common to agents who consistently achieve their revenue and quality-of-life goals.

1. Set a daily time and place for prospecting

You can't work your prospecting around your day. You have to work your day around your prospecting. You have to establish the habit and engage in the discipline of prospecting on a daily basis and from a controlled environment where your prospecting tools are available and readily accessible.

I often ask agents who are just starting or have renewed their focus for prospecting, "When does prospecting happen during your day?" I can see they made their contacts, but what I really want to know is did the contacts happen during a scheduled prospecting time, or did they just "gut it out"? My definition of "gutting it out" is just doing it because of sheer desire, commitment, discipline, or will. That's better than not completing the prospecting, but it's not sustainable in the long run. Somewhere along your ride to success, the will to do it will have to be replaced with the habit of doing it.

In my private office, I set up a prospecting station that included a stand-up area, a computer, and a telephone with a headset. Tacked on one wall were scripts for use when contacting expired-listing and FSBO prospects, past clients, those in my sphere of influence, and those whom I reached via cold calls. On another wall I posted all my objection-handling scripts, including a few options for each objection. This kept me prepared for any dialogue or direction the conversation took and helped me avoid fumbles.

Knowing that body language makes up 55 percent of the power of communication, even when communicating by phone, I kept my intensity and focus high by standing up. The headset — which I consider an absolutely essential prospecting tool — enabled me to keep my hands free so I could gesture or accentuate points as if I was speaking directly to my prospect in person.

When making an investment in a headset, don't get the cheapest one you can find. Spend a few hundred dollars to get one of high quality. Otherwise, you'll end up with such poor sound quality that your prospect won't be able to hear you clearly, hardly a formula for prospecting success.

2. Fight off distractions

The truth is, most agents welcome distractions that take them away from prospecting obligations. An inbound phone call, a text message, a social-media message or post, a problem transaction, a home-inspection question, an incoming email, an agent who wants to talk, anything will do. It's called creative avoidance, and agents generally excel at the art.

Whether you're just starting out or you're a top agent in your market, distractions never just go away. Real estate professionals face more distractions than ever because of the access and technology driving the real estate industry. In fact, the best agents have even more potential for distraction because of the volume of business, the number of staff people, the size of client transactions, and the scope of responsibilities they juggle. The difference between prospecting avoidance and prospecting success comes down to the question, what do you do when the distractions hit? Do you postpone prospecting while you put out a fire? Do you decide to make just a few calls to settle the pending issue? Do you justify not starting your prospecting at the appointed time? If you said "yes" to any of those questions, you're practicing creative avoidance.

To fight off distractions, you have to bar their access:

Turn off your email, so the "you've got mail" icon doesn't tempt you.

Ask the receptionist to take messages for inbound calls during your prospecting session.

Turn off your cellphone.

Close down social-networking sites.

Put a sign on the door that basically says, "Don't bother me; I'm prospecting."

Tell anyone who asks for a meeting during your prospecting period that you already have an appointment, because you are working to find a potential prospect.

3. Follow the plan

Success boils down to taking the right steps in the proper order.

To get your prospecting steps and order correct, you must follow a prospecting plan. You must know who you're going to call and for what reason. The best approach is to set up each day's prospecting plan a day in advance.

If you wait to put your prospecting plan together at the beginning of your prospecting session, chances are too high that you'll talk yourself out of more calls than you make. Your mental process will get in the way of action, causing you to think things like "This person will think I'm calling back too soon " or "This person won't buy or sell right now."

If you establish a plan in advance, you'll be ready for action instead of second-guessing. Follow these steps:

1. Do your research; establish your plan and set up for the next day's prospecting one day in advance. Before you leave your office for the day, determine the prospecting calls you're going to make the next day. Assemble everything you'll need for the calls and put the information on your desk so it's ready for your attention as soon as you walk in the door.

2. In the morning, quickly review your calls and daily goals. A word of caution: Don't take too long! You could be setting yourself up for creative avoidance.

3. Spend 20 minutes practicing scripts, dialogues, and objection-handling techniques. Establish a pre-call routine and create a pattern or plan that you repeat over and over again before each prospecting session or call.

As an analogy, think of how other professionals warm up before performances. Whether you're watching musicians, actors, or athletes, you expect them to be fully prepared and ready to go when their concerts, plays, or games begin. Follow the same rule. Warm up in advance so that by the time you pick up the phone, practice is over and you're ready for the real thing.

4. Review a few affirmations, such as

- "I'm a great prospector."

- "When I prospect, people love to talk with me and set appointments with me."

- "I will generate leads and appointments before I'm through today."

You're now ready to pick up the phone with focus, intensity, and an expectation of success.

5. Be faithful to yourself and finish what you start

Stay faithful to your daily objectives by completing all your prospecting contacts down to the very last one.

When you're running a race, you have to run the whole way. No one remembers who was ahead at the 80-meter mark of the men's 100-meter race at the Olympics. The winner has to complete the full circuit before he can claim his medal. Don't drop out early; finish what you start.

You can work harder. Or you can work smarter.

Most successful agents don't go into a secluded room, pick up the phone, and toil away making hundreds of random calls over a nonstop eight-hour period. Few people would even consider that approach. I know I wouldn't, and I doubt you would.

Instead, those who win at prospecting begin by targeting who they will call and why. They don't waste their time or effort calling iffy contacts that may or may not even be in the real estate market.

Prospecting is only effective if it generates a lead from a truly qualified prospect, someone who is interested in what you offer, needs the service you provide, and has the ability and authority to become a client of your business, or to refer you to someone who could.

Setting and achieving prospecting goals

In setting prospecting goals, focus on three core areas: the number of contacts you should make each day and week, the number of leads you should develop, and the number of personal appointments you should set.

Start with easily attainable numbers so you can build up your energy, intensity, focus, and discipline slowly and steadily. You wouldn't run a marathon without working up your daily and weekly mileage over time, and the same premise applies when establishing and meeting your prospecting goals.

Number of contacts made

A contact is a personal conversation with a decision maker who can make a purchase or sale or refer you to someone who can. A contact is not a conversation with the babysitter, a ten-year-old neighbor, a friendly teenager, or an answering machine.

When I take on a new coaching client, I almost always start them with a goal of five contacts a day, and I suggest the same for you. Make a goal of 5 contacts a day without fail, resulting in the completion of 25 contacts a week.

It will take three to four weeks for contact with five prospects a day to become a habit. After you achieve the goal for three consecutive weeks without missing a single workday, you can raise your goal to seven or ten.

Number of leads established

Leads are contacts that have demonstrated through their dialogues that they possess the basic motivation and desire to make a change in their living arrangements. In prospecting, we have to make some assumptions until we either pre-qualify a client ourselves or they secure an appointment with a lender that determines they have the financial capacity to make a purchase.

To advance your business, aim to develop at least one lead per day and five leads per week.

Number of appointments secured

An appointment is a face-to-face meeting with prospects, during which you discuss their needs and wants, share how you work, and aim to gain their commitment to work with you in an exclusive relationship to sell their home or find them a home to purchase. An appointment is the launch of the agent-client relationship. It's not a meeting during which you show a property.

Like your lead-generation goal, your appointment goal should be set at a reasonable level: A goal of one appointment a week is a solid start. If you acquire two appointments, terrific, but make sure that you're able to secure at least one.

If you're thinking, "Hmm, five leads and only one appointment a week from all those calls . . . ," realize that these are starting goals. It's far better to begin with aims you can actually achieve rather than ones that overwhelm you from the onset. As you gain consistency and skill in prospecting, both your numbers and your ratios will improve.

Even if you only maintain the starting goals, you'll have a good year as a newer agent. At the end of the year, you will have made 1,250 contacts and created 250 leads. You also will have set and conducted 50 appointments and gotten two weeks off with your family to boot.

Even if only half of the appointments turn into listings or sales, you'll have 25 deals in your first year. In most companies, that will make you rookie of the year. You'll also earn in excess of $125,000 in gross commission income. I don't know too many people in real estate or in any other profession who make that type of money in their first year.

Using Craigslist for lead generation

Craigslist has become an effective marketing tool for many real estate agents. You receive a wide variety of leads from Craigslist postings. The goal of using Craigslist with IDX is to create an IDX registration or inbound inquiry from your Craigslist ad.

In Craigslist, you want to post ads frequently. When a new ad gets posted, your ad is pushed downward; posting frequently puts your ad back toward the top of the list. You also need to change your ad copy so Craigslist doesn't view it as a duplicate, or what it calls "ghosting."

Post ads in multiple price ranges and geographic locations. Only a small group of real estate agents uses Craigslist regularly, which means more opportunities for you. You can post your company listings in addition to your own, as long as you get permission from your broker manager or the other agents in your office to post their properties. You can also gain permission pretty easily from real estate companies that are fixed fee or low fee. Their sales margins are much lower, so they usually invest limited dollars and time in marketing their properties. Your Craigslist ad needs to drive buyers to more detailed information about the property, as well as your IDX options. This means more leads and prospects for you.

Using enhanced lead-generation systems

Many different lead-generation systems can support and expand on your IDX system. These systems can also connect with your Craigslist ads, pay-per- click campaigns, and other forms of marketing. Many of these systems help with search-engine placement, but the biggest benefit is conversion of the leads you generate. Systems like BoomTown, TigerLead, Kunversion, Realty Generator, Zurple, Real Geeks, and others like them can help you better manage and convert your leads.

These systems also provide better service to your clients and prospects than most basic MLS IDX systems. They enable consumers to track, moni- tor, and save properties they mark as favorites. As with a standard MLS IDX, they enable online prospects to set up specific search parameters that notify them instantly when a new property that matches their criteria comes on the market.

Most of these services, unlike the basic MLS IDX systems, have a smart-drip campaign that sends targeted messages to prospects at intervals based on their level of activity on the site and on what they're searching for. As an agent, you have all that information compiled in your dashboard, so you can view all the prospect's actions and favorite properties. The final component of most systems is a CRM (client relationship management) solution. This creates a closed-loop system to manage both your lead generation and lead conversion.

Building stealth sites

One good strategy is to develop stealth sites where your personal branding isn't so prominently displayed. Most states require your name, your com- pany name, and your contact information to be displayed on the site, but if a user has to scroll all the way down to see it, she probably won't. This gives the website the appearance of a free service. This strategy creates the perception of a "salesperson-free site." It makes prospects more comfort- able and less hesitant to register when asked to. This can increase your lead volume and conversion rates.

You can build multiple stealth landing pages inexpensively to deliver your IDX offer. For each landing page, secure a website address that will be powerful in both search-engine optimization and pay-per-click campaigns. For example, you can target Seattle buyers interested in foreclosed properties with a landing page with URL that speaks to a target audience can drive traffic.

CHAPTER TEN

Work Your Sphere Of Influence

First, realize that you already have a sphere of influence, You have family, friends, old schoolmates, previous business associates, soccer buddies, and more. These are people that know you, and just because of that, you have some influence on them.

Throughout your career in real estate, you should always have a plan to grow this group and implement it faithfully. It will become a huge source of repeat and referral business over time.

Get Your Current List All in One Place

This is a big task, but it's important and begs planning to avoid duplicate work later. You'll be surprised at how large a list you can come up with when you start pulling in your friends, old classmates, sports team members, business associates, your doctor, lawyer, and others.

What is important is to hopefully start with something more than a list on paper. If you use Outlook in your computer, use the contacts database or another like it to get these people into a system for management. Today's technology and Client Relationship Management (CRM) software and online systems make this a much easier and more efficient task.

Make Contact the Way You Usually Do

You want to communicate effectively but also save some money. There are plenty of advisors out there that will have you develop a really nice letter in envelopes and mail via first-class mail. This may be how you do it for some of your lists.

However, if you're making a really large contact list, many of them will be people you usually talk to via email, text messaging, or phone. It's OK to contact them the way you always have. Just split your list into groups by contact method.

Categorize Your List by How You Know Your Contacts

As you progress in your career and your knowledge of contact management, you'll find that you want to have certain common types by which to identify contacts. Go ahead and start working toward that now. If you're using Outlook, you can use the "Categories" function for this.

You would have categories for Friends, Family, Vendors (doctor, lawyer, local grocer,etc.), Buyer Prospect, Seller Prospect, etc. The buyer and seller prospect categories are for those new ones you're about to get. Segment your contacts and prospects into logical groups that you would market to in specific ways.

Develop Your Announcement and Send it Out

If you're contacting via several methods, such as some email and some phone, develop scripts for each, letting them know about your new business. It's as simple as: "Hi XYZ, I've started a new career and wanted to let you know about it. I've gotten my license and I'm now a real estate agent with XYZ Brokerage in town. Please give me a boost by thinking of me if you're planning a real estate transaction or recommending me to those you know." Don't forget your contact info.

Whatever you do, if you get a response, you need to reply back to them and thank them. You're beginning a relationship that can lead to money in the bank, so start it out on the right foot.

Plan Ongoing Contact and Do It!

Now that you've sent out your "new agent career" announcement to your SOI, make a plan for how often you want to contact them. This can vary by type, such as family will not need a lot of follow-ups. Follow the plan and make regular contact. There's nothing worse than finding out a good friend bought a home elsewhere because they forgot about that first announcement a year ago.

Do Some Quick List-Building Activities

Get started immediately in adding to your sphere of influence list. Get involved in community activities, go to homeowner association meetings, give out your business card to the person behind the dry cleaner counter. If you go for coffee in the mornings alone, stop getting a table and sit at the counter. Strike up a conversation with the person next to you.

Sphere Of Influence Criteria

Think about how many people may be aware of you. If you have any kind of online presence, a large number of people may be listening to your message. They may not know you all that well or even trust you, but you have the potential to influence them. With this in mind, here is the criteria I use to determine if somebody is in my sphere of influence:

1. DO THEY KNOW ME?

Keep in mind that this does not just refer to people I have met in person. I could have spoken to somebody over the phone or messaged an internet lead. In other words, all this takes is some kind of introduction.

2. DO I WANT TO DO BUSINESS WITH THEM?

You know as well as I do that not everybody you meet is going to be an ideal client. For this very reason, I take the time to think about whether the person is somebody I want to be working with before deciding if they belong on my sphere-of-influence list.

3. AM I WILLING TO INVEST TIME TO GET TO KNOW THEM BETTER?

This is super important: if I were to add somebody to my sphere list and never talk to them again, they'd soon forget about me. This means I'd have little to no influence over them.

To meet this requirement, you need to implement a sphere marketing program where you contact everybody on at least a quarterly basis. For instance, I use Sphere Influencer, which reminds me to nurture relationships for the maximum impact.

How To Expand Your Sphere Of Influence

- Find Your Way Around Facebook

An easy way to see a sphere of influence in action is to use Facebook as a social media platform. Consider the current contacts in your sphere and connect with them via Facebook. Build connections with friends, family, neighbors, co-workers, local businesses, and more. Be interactive, commenting on their posts as well as posting on the account. Include personalized content as well as professional updates to build authentic relationships with your connections. Want to expand your sphere further? Get connected on Twitter and LinkedIn, too. Remember to use relevant, keyword-based tags on social media to help more people find you.

- Send a Message

Staying in touch with connections is crucial to maintaining a sphere of influence and bring more people into the circle. Find out the best way to communicate with people, then offer to send updates via email or text message. Include links to updated listings, current housing market information, and announcements about upcoming events in the community. Mix up the messages to give recipients a reason to open them.

- Maximize the Power of Printed Materials

Traditional methods, such as distributing printed materials, continue to be productive today. Agents should always have business cards handy to give to everyone they meet. A sleek, printed brochure is a professional addition to any open house. Flyers about the neighborhood and basic real estate information are helpful to distribute at community centers and houses of worship throughout the area. Sending direct mail pieces is another great way to connect with clients.

- Sponsor a Charitable Event

Agents need to put their names in front of the community, so people remember them when they are ready to buy or sell a property. One way to stay at the forefront of local news is to sponsor a charitable event. Some agents sponsor a sports team while others get involved with neighborhood causes, such as raising money for a family in need. Supporting the community helps agents gain trust and recognition.

- Become an Information Speaker

Local groups, such as libraries and senior citizen centers, always look for informational speakers to attend their meetings. Create sessions about buying and selling property to appeal to the specific group. Speaking at events helps agents establish themselves as recognized authorities in the local real estate industry. Other engagements and referrals are sure to follow a successful event.

- Attend a Regional Networking Events

Continuing education is crucial for real estate agents to remain relevant and to thrive in a continually evolving marketplace. Networking events provide essential industry updates and give agents a golden opportunity to connect with other professionals. Building a robust professional network enables agents to refer their clients to people they trust. And, these professionals will also send referrals to an agent, helping to generate more leads. Better Homes and Gardens Real Estate agents have access to the Be Better University for outstanding professional development.

- Communicate through Pictures

Creating and maintaining a sphere of influence relies on secure communication. Agents need to connect with people in a meaningful way, so they are remembered. For those who struggle with words, photos can be an excellent way to connect in the real estate industry. Post listings and personal images to sites such as Pinterest and Instagram to reach out to your connections. Share and comment on the photos posted by your contacts to encourage interactive relationships. Use professional imagery to attract attention and promote interest in your listings.

Expanding your sphere of influence requires communication, interaction, and authentic connections. From social media to local events, there are countless ways to connect with other individuals and businesses to increase your sphere. As agents establish and maintain more meaningful connections, they will steadily generate more leads.

CHAPTER ELEVEN

Track Everything In A Database

As a real estate agent, you have to be able to keep in touch with prospects and clients easily and effectively. You must be able to put your hands on names, addresses, phone numbers, and email addresses in an instant.

You can track people and prospects using the old-fashioned way, on 3x5 note cards, but you'll soon outgrow that method. My advice is to get a client relationship management (CRM) software package. Many, such as Sage ACT, GoldMine, and Salesforce, are specifically designed for salespeople. These programs automate your client database, sales, and more.

Another option is to buy service that is specific to the real estate industry. The programs that are specific to real estate agents hold many advantages over general sales programs. They're usually programmed with letters and correspondence an agent can use. They also have pre-created lead follow-up and client follow-up plans already built in. Most have plans to apply when marketing a property. They also have plans you can launch after you've secured a buyer for a listing.

I recommend real estate-specific software like Top Producer, Wise Agent, or RealtyJuggler. Most of these programs are web-based, which means they can be accessed from anywhere or from any tool, such as a computer, laptop, tablet, or smartphone. Additionally, most charge a monthly fee. This allows you to pay as you go rather than budgeting for a large upfront cost, and you get the updates for free.

A good contact management system is a must for any serious agent. Most agents attempt to use Outlook. This is wrong! In my opinion, Outlook doesn't have the necessary power and lacks the "cascading action plans." You need to be able to set a lead follow-up or contact sequence and automate the process of reaching out to clients and prospects.

Finding Safety and Success in Numbers

Sales is a Numbers Game.

Prospecting is a numbers game, as well. The problem is, too few agents actually know their numbers and how to track them.

It help you understand and set objectives for your ratios of contacts to leads, leads to closings, appointments to contracts, and contracts to closings. Knowing this information moves you almost immediately into the league of our industry's most productive agents.

The Law of Accumulation

The law of accumulation basically says that achievement is the result of ongoing and constant effort. Everything in life, whether positive or negative, compounds itself over time.

An illustration of this is money. If you want to be a millionaire, all you have to do is save a little on a consistent basis, and the law of accumulation will take over.

If you put away $2.74 a day from the time you are 20 until you are 65 and receive an average rate of return of 9 percent over those years, you'll be a millionaire. You will have saved about $45,000 over those 45 years; the law of accumulation does the rest. If you ask most people whether they'll trade $45,000 for $1 million, they'll say yes, but few people actually make the effort.

You can expect an equally uneven return when you invest in prospecting.

The tricky part is that the reward for your miniscule investment of prospecting effort doesn't happen overnight. You have to prospect for 90 days before the law of accumulation does its thing. As my good friend says, "Life is like a cafeteria. First you pay, and then you get to eat."

The Power of Consistency

Marginally successful agents take a binge approach to prospecting. Highly successful agents are far, far more consistent in their efforts.

The Never-Ending Prospecting Cycle

Agents can easily find time to prospect when they have no listings, no pending transactions, and no buyers to work with.

The secret is to continue to prospect even when you're busy with all the other activities.

Look at a typical agent's annual income stream and you'll see that it goes up and down like a yoyo. Most agents have four to six good income months per year. If you overlay their revenue streams with their prospecting numbers, you'll see that revenue decreases when prospecting tapers off, leading directly to the business void that follows.

Your job as a real estate agent is to fill a pipeline of leads so you always have new prospects to work with. And the only way to keep a healthy pipeline or conveyer belt of leads is to prospect consistently.

The importance of tracking results

Any business in sales can be broken down to a series of repeatable numbers that, over time, produce a pre-determined result. When you establish goals and track your performance over a few months, you can determine the activities you need to earn the income you desire.

As a real estate agent, I decided that I needed one appointment per day in order to reach my income goal. I knew through tracking my numbers that I needed three leads to create one appointment. What's more, I knew I needed to make twelve contacts to generate one high-quality lead because, through monitoring my numbers, I knew that two of every three leads would be "tire kickers" contacts who didn't have the desire, need, ability, or authority to either list or buy in the reasonably near future.

The law of averages evens out your numbers over time. Don't evaluate yourself on a single day's achievements. Even a week is too short a period for evaluation. I've had days when I didn't set a single appointment. I probably had weeks that I got skunked. During a three-month period, however, I was always within a 5 percent margin of error on my number.

Staying in Touch

Use your contact-management system to trigger the next call to a prospect and make staying in touch automatic and easy.

Each time you end a prospecting call, determine when the next call will take place. Find your prospect's timeframe and when you should speak again. Then schedule the contact right then and there.

When talking to a past client or sphere member, schedule the next call without even asking. Then, the next time you call, they'll be pleasantly surprised to hear from you.

In addition to making calls, send emails to thank contacts for their time and to reiterate your service offer.

Get permission to add contacts to your blog or email newsletter mailing.

Follow up first-time contacts with a copy of your agency brochure or marketing piece. Or send a "Just listed" or "Just sold" card to demonstrate your success as an agent.

Craft a personalized business letter, perfectly typed onto your letterhead and sent out in your matching envelope.

Most of us get hundreds of emails a day, most of which we don't even want. We receive hundreds of pieces of junk mail a month, mostly from credit-card and mortgage-refinance companies.

The handwritten thank-you note breaks through the clutter. It looks like an invitation to something special. It enhances the personal relationship and keeps it active until you talk again in a few days. It's still the best way to keep in touch in our technology-driven world.